PRAISE FOR *CALM CURE*

'Imagine our planet free of war. Imagine your life free
of conflict. World peace is possible through inner
peace in each of us. I am deeply inspired by Sandy
Newbigging's pioneering work with Mind
Calm, Body Calm *and now* Calm Cure.'
ROBERT HOLDEN, AUTHOR OF *SHIFT HAPPENS!* AND *HAPPINESS NOW!*

'Calm Cure *is a beautiful oasis of relief for the restless and
frustrated mind, as it brings about resolution to the hidden
conflicts that keep us from living in harmony, happiness
and peace. Reading it is a gift to your spirit and will lead
you to creating all that your heart truly desires.'*
SONIA CHOQUETTE, AUTHOR OF *YOUR 3 BEST SUPER POWERS*

'Sandy shows that once we remove our inner conflict
we are better able to have great relationships, success
in our careers, an abundance of money, more time and
even impact the wider world in a more honest, real and
powerful way. I wholeheartedly recommend this book!'
DAVID HAMILTON, AUTHOR OF *HOW YOUR MIND CAN HEAL YOUR BODY*

'In today's changing world this is a must-read for those
committed to living a peaceful, grounded life.'
REBECCA CAMPBELL, AUTHOR OF *LIGHT IS THE NEW BLACK*
AND *RISE SISTER RISE*

'Sandy encourages us to stop fighting ourselves and to stop
fighting life. The inner peace that this leads to will manifest
as outer peace in both our physical bodies and the wider
world. What could be more relevant nowadays than that?'
CHARLIE MORLEY, AUTHOR OF

'Calm Cure *introduces you to exceptional tools to stimulate healing of your mind, body and soul.*'
PHIL PARKER, AUTHOR OF *THE LIGHTNING PROCESS*®

'*Sandy does it again, but more deeply and profoundly than ever before. This book gets to the heart of the matter and allows you to go deeper into your true natural state of beingness, and becoming free of emotional and physical conflict. Thank you, Sandy, for sharing your profound knowledge; the world needs to read this book!*'
JOSEPH CLOUGH, AUTHOR OF *BE YOUR POTENTIAL*

'Calm Cure *guides us to release what we are convinced that we want in order to receive so much more of what we actually need. There's an abundance and a flow that wants to move through us and inform our actions, and Sandy shows us the way to unlock it.*'
MEGGAN WATTERSON, AUTHOR OF *REVEAL* AND *HOW TO LOVE YOURSELF*

'*I love the shift that Sandy talks about in* Calm Cure*, moving from the "fix it" perspective to the "peace with" perspective. Most of the stress we experience is around the pressure we put on ourselves to control or change a situation. Sandy's technique is straightforward and his outlook on life is soothing. The world needs more calm – and this could be the book to help you get there.*'
ABBY WYNNE, AUTHOR OF *HOW TO BE WELL*

'*What I love about Sandy is his passion and commitment to helping others heal and reconnect to who they truly are. With* Calm Cure*, Sandy has done it again – he has poured his heart and soul into writing this book and I'm excited for everyone who picks it up and follows his process.*'
BRETT MORAN, AUTHOR OF *WAKE THE F*CK UP*

CALM CURE

BY THE SAME AUTHOR

BOOKS

*Body Calm: The Powerful Meditation Technique
That Helps Your Body Heal and Stay Healthy*

*Mind Calm: The Modern-Day Meditation Technique
that Gives You 'Peace with Mind'*

Thunk! How to Think Less for Serenity and Success

Heal the Hidden Cause: With the 5-Step Mind Detox Method

*Life Detox: Clear Physical and Emotional
Toxins from Your Body and Your Life*

*New Beginnings: Ten Teachings for Making the
Rest of Your Life the Best of Your Life*

CD/DIGITAL DOWNLOAD

*Body Calm Meditations: Experience the Power of
Meditation for Self-Healing and Superb Health*

*Mind Calm Meditations: Experience the Serenity
and Success that Come from Thinking Less*

CALM CURE

THE UNEXPECTED WAY TO IMPROVE YOUR HEALTH, YOUR LIFE AND YOUR WORLD

SANDY C. NEWBIGGING

HAY HOUSE

Carlsbad, California • New York City • London
Sydney •Johannesburg • Vancouver • New Delhi

Copyright © 2017 by Sandy C. Newbigging

Published and distributed in the United States by: Hay House, Inc.: www.hayhouse.com®
• **Published and distributed in Australia by:** Hay House Australia Pty. Ltd.: www.hayhouse.com
.au • **Published and distributed in the United Kingdom by:** Hay House UK, Ltd.: www.hayhouse
.co.uk • **Published and distributed in the Republic of South Africa by:** Hay House SA (Pty),
Ltd.: www.hayhouse.co.za • **Distributed in Canada by:** Raincoast Books: www.raincoast.com
• **Published in India by:** Hay House Publishers India: www.hayhouse.co.in

Cover design: Kari Brownlie • *Interior design:* Leanne Siu Anastasi • *Interior images:* iStockphoto

All rights reserved. No part of this book may be reproduced by any mechanical, photographic,
or electronic process, or in the form of a phonographic recording; nor may it be stored in a
retrieval system, transmitted, or otherwise be copied for public or private use—other than
for "fair use" as brief quotations embodied in articles and reviews—without prior written
permission of the publisher.

The author of this book does not dispense medical advice or prescribe the use of any
technique as a form of treatment for physical, emotional, or medical problems without the
advice of a physician, either directly or indirectly. The intent of the author is only to offer
information of a general nature to help you in your quest for emotional, physical, and spiritual
well-being. In the event you use any of the information in this book for yourself, the author
and the publisher assume no responsibility for your actions.

Library of Congress Control Number: 2017933248

Tradepaper ISBN: 978-1-4019-5335-5

10 9 8 7 6 5 4 3 2 1
1st edition, May 2017

Printed in the United States of America

To M.K.I.

'If you argue with "what is" you will suffer. Period.'
MAHARISHI KRISHNANANDA ISHAYA (M.K.I.)

CONTENTS

FOREWORD

I first began studying the mind–body connection while working as a research and development scientist with one of the world's largest pharmaceutical companies. Fascinated by the placebo effect, I began to investigate how the mind – in particular, attitudes, emotions and beliefs – affected the body.

In placebo research, it is now very well understood that a person's belief, or expectation, alters their brain chemistry in a way consistent with what they expect to happen. Even placing attention on any part of the body will activate the corresponding brain region, which then sends signals to the part of the body being focused upon. In a real sense, energy flows where attention goes.

It is also now well known that focusing the mind on the breath during meditation causes physical changes in brain matter and turns activity up or down in over 1,500 genes. A feeling of love can flood the arteries with oxytocin, a cardioprotective hormone that can reduce blood pressure. On the other hand, focusing on things that annoy us can flood the body with stress hormones instead.

The mind exerts a powerful effect on the body. Once thought of as just something that we interpret the world with and use to make a few decisions, the mind can now even be thought of as a force in that our thoughts, emotions and beliefs exert an actual force on our biology.

The mental practice of visualization has been shown to cause physical changes in the brain through neuroplasticity. Research and practice has been expanded to help people recover faster from stroke or sporting injuries, and many top sports people even spend time every day visualizing themselves at their best, knowing that doing so actually exerts an effect on their muscles.

There is now no question that the mind impacts the body. One of the things I love about Sandy Newbigging's work is that he helps people to discover if there is a link between current symptoms of illness or injury and their thoughts, emotions, beliefs or assumptions and, if so, shows them how to heal by first finding peace in their mind. The idea is that if the state of the body is somehow mirroring the condition of the mind, then once the mind moves towards peace, so the mirrored state in the body may change such that the body then moves towards wellness.

I find Sandy's Calm Cure method very powerful for when there seems to be a psychological link. I decided to try it out on myself, having felt frustrated by a lingering muscle strain that was preventing me from playing sports. Following Sandy's method, I identified an area where I felt torn in my life, then made peace with it by identifying what my attachment was and what I was resisting. I was pleasantly surprised that after finding some peace with my inner conflict, I was swiftly back exercising again.

While researching through scientific journals in the writing of my own books I have, from time to time, found research indicating a correlation between a person's psychological state or emotional expression and some illnesses or diseases.

For example, some research suggests that hostility, which can be thought of as expressed contempt, is linked with coronary artery calcification – a form of hardening of the arteries – in some people. In a sense, as we harden emotionally so we harden on the inside too, almost as if the biological state is a mirror of the emotional state.

Research by Lydia Temoshok, while at the University of California School, San Francisco, found a link between Type-C personality and the thickness of certain tumours. Type-C personality is characterized by suppressing negative emotion. It's almost as if pushing negative emotion down, which can cause it to grow in intensity, was mirrored in the growth of the tumour.

On the other hand, research by James Pennebaker, social psychology professor at the University of Texas at Austin, has shown that releasing stored negative emotion by simply writing about past hurts can elevate a person's immune response to pathogens. Similarly, forgiveness has been shown to reduce blood pressure and increase blood flow to the heart. Stored negative emotion, and therefore stress, seems to correlate with illness, while releasing the emotion or finding some peace seems to be health giving.

Perhaps some of the most exciting recent research is where both meditation and emotional expression and support were found to offset the loss of telomere length in the cells of breast cancer survivors. Telomeres are end caps on DNA that help stop it unravelling. They are vital to the life of a cell, but they gradually wear down, in part due to the stresses and strains of life. So, in other words, meditation and the release of negative emotion was having an actual protective effect on cells.

Given the growing understanding of the mind–body connection and how it can be harnessed to improve health, I believe that Sandy Newbigging has made an exciting and very important contribution to the field.

Calm Cure goes further. We all want to be kind and love ourselves, others, and life; we also have goals, hopes, dreams and aspirations. Regardless of our focus, however, our conditioning can get in the way. Sandy draws some intelligent conclusions about our relationships with ourself and the world, and shows how, by simply realigning some of our thinking, we can literally take control of our personal state of peace and happiness, and our personal experiences of reality.

In this book, he addresses how mind and emotions impact our relationships, careers, money, time and even how we feel about, and the impact we have upon, the wider world. It is almost as if our world, from our personal world to the wider world, is an extension of the body, so just as inner conflict impacts the body, so it impacts our lives.

Sandy shows that once we remove our inner conflict in each of these areas, we are better able to have great relationships, success in our careers, a steady flow of and abundance of money, more time and even impact the wider world in a more honest, real and powerful way.

I believe that the many examples Sandy shares in this book will speak directly to readers, as they did to me. We can see the inner conflicts of the people featured in these examples as our own inner conflicts. As Sandy takes us through a step-by-step process for releasing these inner conflicts, we are set free to be more effective in almost any area of our life that we focus upon.

I wholeheartedly recommend this book!

David R. Hamilton PhD
Author of *How Your Mind Can Heal Your Body*
and *The Five Side Effects of Kindness*

ACKNOWLEDGEMENTS

At Hay House I would like to thank Michelle Pilley, Amy Kiberd, Jo Burgess, Julie Oughton, Julie Nolan and Diane Hill in the UK office, and Reid Tracy and Louise Hay in the USA. At Hay House I would also like to thank Tom Cole for helping my books reach so many readers. In addition I would like to thank my excellent editor Sandy Draper for the wonderful work during the edit. Thank you to Kyle Gray, Robert Holden, David Hamilton and the many wonderful Hay House authors for being a constant source of inspiration.

Very special thanks to Maharani. You have been so supportive and instrumental in the final version of this technique and book. You surprise me every day and I love you very much.

I would also like to thank my family – Mum, Dad, Max, Sam and Amber – and every single person that's attended one of my clinics, courses or retreats – including the members of my Calm Clan and growing team of Calmologists. Thank you Suka, Narain, Satta and Bryce for the fun conversations that always stretch my consciousness. Without you all, and the rest of my Ishaya family, this book would not have been possible.

Finally, infinite love and gratitude, as always, go to my Spiritual Teacher, M.K.I. Even during times when I've experienced amnesia from the truth, you've always seen my potential and shown me by your example what it means to live fully and freely.

Introduction

THE UNEXPECTED WAY

Calming Hidden Conflicts

Stop fighting life. It's hurting you, making you sick, ruining your relationships and messing with your money. Hidden conflict creates emotional upset: it stresses us out, makes us a victim of circumstance and stands in the way of lasting satisfaction and success.

It's been said that 'resistance is futile' and it is so true. There is a direct relationship between how much we resist life and the stress and suffering we endure. The more we push against what happens, the more life tends to push back, creating conflict and preventing true peace and prosperity. But if you are willing to muster the courage to lay down arms and cultivate what I call 'peace *with* life', then consistent inner calm, better health, freedom from persistent problems and genuine life success can be your rewards.

Calm Cure invites us to wake up from our conditioning to be in conflict, and transform our relationship with life.

Most of us are so preoccupied with trying to deal with, and treat, the symptoms of our problems that we never get around to discovering and resolving the underlying causes. Anytime you have a physical condition or life problem there are always three parts at play; however, we are taught to focus only on the first two.

Let me explain. If you have a physical condition then you will have a name for it (migraines, for example), and it will have been diagnosed because of certain symptoms (headaches, nausea, etc.). Similarly, if you have a life problem, it too will have a name (financial issues, for instance) plus its associated symptoms (debt, stress, sleepless nights, etc.). But if you look a little deeper, you will find in both cases that there is also a third element – what I call the 'conflict experience'. This is how it feels within you to be living with the condition or problem, which is reflecting an *experience* in your life that you don't want and are therefore in *conflict* with.

What you'll discover in the following chapters is that we can heal and achieve almost anything by bringing calm to where there has been conflict.

A FRUITLESS FIGHT

We have been conditioned to be in a battle with life. To resist anything that doesn't go our way, show up how we want, meet our high hopes or satisfy our eternal hunger for more, better and improved. We have been conditioned to be attached to what we believe will make us happy and end up frustrated or upset when life doesn't match our expectations. We have been conditioned to feel bad, get stressed and end up sick – due to having chronic unconscious conflicts *with* life. But don't get disheartened; it doesn't need to be this way. There is a way to clarify and clear the conflicts that are the undercover culprits of our health conditions, persistent life problems and untapped potential.

Calm Cure brings conscious calm to anywhere in your life that there is unconscious conflict. Giving us the opportunity to be liberated from the constraints of the conditioning that causes us to be engaged in a fruitless fight with life. It achieves this by empowering us with the life-changing ability to rise above reactive resistances and ascend beyond unseen attachments, which you will learn are the two core components of any conflict. Ultimately providing us with the priceless skill to possess an unshakable peace *with* life, irrespective of what's happened in the past, is happening today or might happen in the future.

> *Your relationship with life has a massive impact on how peaceful, healthy, wealthy, happy and successful you are.*

Loving life and living free from prolonged stress and suffering is possible. Not necessarily by endlessly working to fix, change and improve everything that is contrary to our personal preferences, but by healing our relationship *with* life. This approach requires us to open up to the possibility that it is not what's happening, but our relationship *with* what's happening that matters more. Knowing this, you can make the heroic choice to stop the struggle and do the inner work required to bring calm to any conflict within yourself and towards life. Make this all-important shift, and I promise the quality of your life experience will start improving in unexpected ways.

A SURPRISING SOLUTION

Although we can't always control what happens during daily life, we can heal the habit of harbouring disharmony *with* what happens. In doing so, we can enjoy emotional ease, holistic health and genuine life success. Having a healthier relationship *with* life stops harmful forms of stress in their tracks and gives us a consistent state of calm that is no longer dependent on circumstance.

You can help your body to heal through enhanced inner harmony and improve your relationships by connecting instead of conflicting. You can be financially free, no longer feel squeezed by time and make a massive impact in your chosen career. All of this is possible by making one simple choice – calm over conflict – and this book will show you how.

Calm Cure is unapologetically uncomplicated. It has taken more than 15 years of research, countless clinical cases and thousands of hours of personal meditation to get to a point where I can share this supremely simple way of improving your life. But it is worth noting that there is a high probability that you'll need to adopt a new strategy; one that may be the polar opposite to anything you've tried before. I'm going to suggest that the best, quickest and most enjoyable way to change anything for the better is to stop being in conflict with how it is now. Or said differently, to take a time out from working so hard, trying to fix everything you believe is wrong about your mind, emotions, body or life, and be at peace with the current reality of how things are. I know this may sound counterproductive. Surely, if you don't work to change things then life will stay the same? With the right attitude and approach, you can discover that the opposite happens.

*Problems continue
until you cure the hidden conflict.*

Time after time, I have found that conflict keeps us connected to the very things that we don't want. The more we resist, the more what we don't want tends to persist. The more we are attached to things being different, the more the underlying fear-based intentions have a way of repelling the very things we want too. But when we are finally willing to experience fully whatever life is presenting to us, then the lack of conflict has a magical way of bringing change, and dare I say it, in ways that are far better than we may have ever imagined possible.

In *Calm Cure*, you'll learn a powerful technique for healing any conditioned conflicts that have been negatively impacting your experience of life and secretly stopping you from living fully and freely. You'll also get guidance on how to apply it to your health, emotions, relationships, career, finances, time and the wider world, allowing you to transform all aspects of your life. Again, not only by aiming to change or improve anything that is contrary to how you think it *should* be, but by possessing the priceless power to be at peace *with* life. I will also share my directory that lists the most common conflicts that I've found to be the hidden causes of 101 physical conditions. Using Calm Cure in daily life you can be peaceful and purposeful, wake up to wellness and enjoy a truly successful life, one that you love.

TOP TIP: FREE ONLINE SUPPORT

At the end of each chapter use the weblink to access additional free resources – no email address required. All the pages are located within a special area of my Calm Clan membership website. You don't have to be a member to access the resources supporting this book; however, if you do choose to join us, then you'll find lots of videos, audios, articles and live broadcasts exclusive to members to help transform your relationship with life.

Part I

THE POWER
OF CALM

Chapter 1

CONFLICT

The Core of Problems

Life is happening. We can't deny it, however hard we might try. There are many opinions on *the purpose of life*. Some say it is to learn how to love or to be of service to our fellow 'man'. Scientists have offered an array of hypotheses, including procreation, survival and evolution of the species, while spiritual teachers have suggested the purpose of life is to 'know thy self' and 'wake up' to enlightenment. All of these purposes are valid, and have merit and relevance here. However, if we begin by bringing it back to basics, without beliefs or opinions, one thing for sure is that *life is happening* and we only get to hang out on this planet for a very limited time. It makes sense, therefore, to aim to experience as much of life as humanly possible.

> *Are you willing to experience all of life,*
> *or just some of it?*

THE SPECTRUM OF LIFE

If gravity and day-to-day life have taught us one thing, it's that although multiple outcomes are possible, what goes up will usually come down, eventually. Rather persistently, life has a way of swinging on a pendulum of possibilities. Sometimes everything will appear to be going great and at other times slide down to the lower end of the desirability scale. Occasionally life will go perfectly to plan and we'll feel in complete control over our destiny, while during other spells an entirely unexpected plot will present itself and life appears to be spinning light years outside our sphere of influence. Some mornings we wake up filled with focus and feel that the universe is our best friend. Other days, the demands of the diary drag us out of bed and it's tricky to put one foot in front of the other without tripping up.

Money may fill your bank account during certain financial periods, then at other times it can feel like the tides have turned and all you do is pay out. Perfect health may be present within you and the people you love during certain stages, and then the onset of a physical condition brings unwanted restraints and scuppers your schedule. Relationships can be on the rise with ample social invitations and so much love and light coming your way that you need to invest in a new pair of Ray Bans. Then before long, you aren't necessarily flavour of the month, with someone somewhere deciding that they no longer like you. Some seasons your team will win and your preferred political party will get voted in, and other seasons... I'm sure by now you get the point. However hard you may try to deny it, life sometimes presents the things you want, the things you don't think you want and everything in between.

Life is happening on a spectrum of possibilities and you aren't failing at being human if it continues to do so.

THE FIX IT, CHANGE IT, IMPROVE IT STRATEGY

What can be done about this tendency of life not always to show up how we would like? One option is to get busy managing, manipulating and controlling every element of existence so that it eventually (and after a hell of a lot of effort) ends up exactly how we want. This strategy involves deciding upon what you believe will make you most happy and then setting about fixing, changing and improving anything that is contrary to your ideal scenario. This approach appears to work, which is probably why millions of people on planet Earth are so busy doing it.

Getting a goal, something you think you want, does feel good. But here's the problem – the good feelings are short-lived and life will send you a curve ball before long. Have you noticed? You can work for ages trying to meet the love of your life or get promoted at work, for example, only to find that the resultant happiness passes much more quickly than the time it took to get it. This everyday predicament is largely due to the foundations of the 'fix it, change it, improve it' strategy being set on conflicted ground.

Conflicted because it buys into the belief (and illusion) that something is wrong with you and your life, and in order to be happy you need something to change. Habitually, if something appears to be wrong, the common reaction is to push it away and if you *need* something different, then you will often end up attached. This strategy causes so much stress and aggravation because of the inner conflict that it inevitably creates.

UNCONSCIOUS CONFLICT

Physical disease, emotional upset and persistent life problems are caused largely by unconscious conflict. Conflict is something that happens within us (on our side of the metaphorical fence) and comes from the opposing inner forces of resistance and attachment. There will be certain elements of our life experience that we don't want, and are therefore resisting, and certain aspects that we think we need instead and are attached to. Until we see this habit, we will often feel the need to fix, change and improve everything *before* we can be completely satisfied. Due to the assumption that once we *do* sort everything out, we will finally find peace, love, happiness and success waiting for us at the end of the 'perfect life' rainbow. Trust me, you won't find what you want there because it's not *what* is happening that makes life feel far from perfect, but an unhealthy relationship *with* life that does. It is the inner conflict – consisting of our reactive resistances due to unacknowledged attachments – that are the primary hidden cause for so much of the stress, dis-ease and discontentment that so many people on this planet suffer from on a daily basis.

> *Conflict is at the core of unhappiness, ill health,*
> *problems and untapped potential.*

Resistance rejects, suppresses, fears, fights and pushes away. Attachment needs, pulls, holds on, controls and, again, fears. When combined the subsequent inner conflict creates stress, tension and eventually, dis-ease within the body. Conflict also causes us to keep recreating the same old life problems over and over, for the simple reason that what we are in conflict with, we remain focused on and magnetized to. Again, until we become aware of this habit, we will spend our days dealing with the symptoms of our conflicts – stress, money worries, relationship disagreements, discontentment, frustration, fear, sadness, etc. Instead of enjoying the inner calm, fulfilment and freedom that are the foundations of holistic health and a wonderful experience of life.

Conditioned to live in conflict

Being in conflict *with* life is a conditioned response and a habit. Over the years, we pick up beliefs from our parents, peers, teachers, advertisers and the mainstream media on the criteria for what a successful human life should look and feel like. What you should do for a living, how much money you should have, the kind of relationships you should hold, how you should look and feel, the holidays you should take, the car you should drive, even the kind of weather that is 'good' and 'bad'... Through the back door, this unconscious conditioning ends up determining what you allow when it happens and what you resist. But don't forget, life is happening on a spectrum of possibilities and all eventualities have the potential of happening at some point.

Life will go to plan sometimes and you will get exactly what you have been conditioned to want. But there will also be occasions when life takes an entirely different path and well, you don't. If you don't calm this conditioning to be in conflict then you can fear what might happen next and waste a huge amount of time, effort

7

and money trying to manage things that sit outside your direct control. Inevitably, your wellbeing will depend upon the weather of whatever life brings. Living this way you will be frustrated and battle your way through life, which is a shame because life can be a delight when we don't treat it like a fight.

THREE ELEMENTS OF EVERY PROBLEM

What has conflict got to do with helping the body heal, bringing resolution to persistent life problems or accessing your full potential during work and play? Everything. Whenever we have an issue, there are three parts at play:

Physical condition	Life problem
Condition **name**	Problem **name**
Physical **symptoms**	Life **symptoms**
Conflict **experience**	Conflict **experience**

Most of the people I meet focus the majority of their attention and efforts on the first two elements: the *name* of their physical condition or life problem and the surface-level *symptoms*. However, there is also always a third element – the conflict experience – that needs to be clarified and calmed. Being aware of all three elements is so important because the conflict experience is more often than not a major contributing factor to the creation and continuation of the physical condition or life problem.

Meaning as long as the unconscious conflict remains chronic, an underlying cause of the issue will remain active. Conflict experiences can be found remarkably easily by investigating how it feels to be living with the condition or problem. In every case I've encountered, the conflict experience is very revealing in uncovering the experience(s) in your external life that you are in conflict with, which you need to get 'peace with' for the physical condition to be healed, life problem transcended or untapped potential freed.

The conflict experience is a life experience that you resist because you're attached to something else happening instead.

Highlighting the hidden cause of conditions

Let's understand this by applying it to a physical condition.

In the case of a rash (condition name), your skin might be red and itchy (physical symptoms). The common response is to reach for a lotion, potion or pill to try to fix the symptoms. But with Calm Cure, you start by describing how the rash makes you feel. You might say, 'Living with this rash makes me feel irritated.' You will then consider where in your life you've felt irritated and what's happening that you don't want: 'I'm feeling irritated because my partner always ignores me by looking at his phone.' With this recognition, you will have found your root-cause resistance of *being ignored*. If there is resistance, then there will be attachment too, which in this case would likely revolve around *being acknowledged*. When combined you will have quickly clarified your conflict experience: the resistance to being ignored and an attachment to being acknowledged – and be well on your way to calming the hidden conflict that has potentially been causing your rash.

Although a skin condition may not be life-threatening, the clarity gained from this approach can be life-saving because the three parts are present in every condition I've come across. Interestingly, you will also discover that the conflict experience will have usually been going on in your life *before* the onset of the health problem. Meaning, conditions are often a symptom of an unrecognized conflict that has remained unseen and unresolved. Using Calm Cure, you can learn to trust your body's wisdom, use physical conditions to highlight unconscious conflicts and be guided towards a harmonious, happier and freer relationship with life.

 **TIP** *Go to www.calmclan.com/conflict for a video on HEALING THE HIDDEN CAUSE.*

Same old life problems, over and over again

When it comes to persistent life problems in your relationships, career, finances, etc., the same principle works wonders.

Let's say that you have money issues (problem name) and you are in debt, lying awake most nights with worry and arguing with your partner over their spending habits (life symptoms). By looking below the surface-level symptoms (insomnia, worry and arguing) to describe your inner experience instead, you may find that your money issues make you feel restricted. You would then explore where feeling restricted has shown up in your life and what's happening that you don't want. 'I often feel restricted around my parents because they always try to make me do what *they* want.' In this case, your root-cause resistance would be *not doing what I want*, with an attachment to *doing what I want*. To calm the conflict experience, you would use the rest of the Calm Cure to get peace with sometimes doing what you want and sometimes not.

Similar to physical conditions being a symptom of conflict, you can discover that your life problems have also been an outer manifestation of inner conflict with certain experiences. Until you do this inner work, you will most likely keep recreating the same external problems and symptoms over and over again. However, if you bring calm to the conflicts that have been keeping you connected to these life patterns, you will see how it creates space within yourself and your life for things to change for the better.

When you resist what you don't want, you keep getting it.
When you calm inner conflicts, new things can enter your life.

ALIGN WITH THE REALITIES OF LIFE

The reality of life is that sometimes what you want will happen and sometimes it won't. You will be loved by some people and judged by others. On time some days and ending up stopped by every red light on other occasions. Calm Cure is therefore not a defeatist or negative approach, but rather one that aligns us with the realities of life. Look outside and you'll see that nature isn't in conflict with the seasons. The trees aren't attached to green leaves or resistant to bare branches. The 'peace with' approach is about aligning with natural law and clearing the conditioning that would cause you to suffer in the face of inevitability.

*Welcome all of life with a wide-open mind
and heart for freedom and fulfilment.*

Calming hidden conflict requires you to be willing to engage in whatever is happening without resistance and attachment. Rather than resisting particular parts of the spectrum of possibilities, the invitation is to cultivate a willingness to experience fully *all* fragrances of life.

Does this sound counterproductive or come across as passive? I mean if you're willing to experience the 'negative' side of the spectrum then surely you will get more of it and the problems in your life or in the world will continue?

In reality this isn't what happens. Resistance repeatedly connects you to what you don't want, whereas being willing to have the life experiences enables them to show up and move on and for new things to come. While attachment often repels what you want or makes you scared of losing what you think you *need*. But when you rise above resistance and appease attachment, inner calm, clarity and contentment follow quickly. You can take whatever action is required, without the negative side effects of conflict. Your body can heal because dis-ease is replaced by inner ease. New life experiences are able to come your way, and you will enjoy a love for your life that is only possible when living with a more all-embracing and unconditional attitude.

How do I experience life fully without suffering?

Responding to this invitation, I often hear, 'OK, so I understand that you are saying I need to stop resisting life and be willing to experience it fully. But how can I do that without opening myself up to lots of emotional turmoil and suffering?'

The good news is that this approach does *not* cause 'negative' emotions, difficult life experiences or suffering because it is conflict towards life that does. We are taught to believe that life is making us feel the way we do, but it is not. It is our relationship with life and whether we welcome or reject what happens that determines how we feel. Meaning, you are experiencing your issue as stressful or problematic because you have been conditioned to resist it. Someone else with a different perspective may experience it as an opportunity and have absolutely no resistance or negative emotions. By not resisting, you can find a surprising amount of peace spontaneously arises within you, because of the absence of conflict.

Calm Cure is not focused on being willing to experience 'negative' emotions, i.e. frustrated or sad. It is focused on cultivating a willingness to engage the full spectrum of life eventualities. When there is no conflict with the life event, we don't tend to feel bad about what's happening.

Let me illustrate the benefits of letting go of conflict with an analogy inspired by my Spiritual Teacher.

Imagine Sam, you and me are together one day and decide to sit beside a road to count the red cars. We find a nearby bench to sit on and start our car-counting game. A few cars pass, a blue one, a silver one and a black one. We just observe them driving past and let them freely come and go. Then we see a red car and count it – one. A few more cars drive by, again we let them, followed by a red car – two. A few more cars pass, including a red one. You and I count it – three. But for some unknown reason, Sam jumps up and starts running as fast as she can up the street – chasing the car – and with a spectacular leap, manages to grab on to the rear bumper of the red car.

You and I look at each other in bemusement as we watch Sam getting dragged up the road behind the red car. By this point, she has lost a shoe, her new jeans are torn and we think we can even see some blood! But if we thought that was peculiar, what comes next takes it to an entire next level.

Sam shouts back at us, 'Guys, this car is hurting me!'

With a desire to help her stop suffering as quickly as possible, we shout back, 'Sam, the car isn't hurting you, holding on to it is. Let it go, let it go!'

Clearly the red car isn't hurting Sam, but rather her struggle from holding on to it. To quickly stop all the hurt, stress and suffering she simply needs to let go.

So how does this work in the real world and within the context of Calm Cure? Something happens that you don't want (a 'red car' experience) and you start resisting it, which connects you to it (i.e. the bumper). As long as you resist it – due to an attachment to something else happening instead – you stay connected to the very thing you don't want and get dragged up the metaphorical street.

'If you argue with "what is" you will suffer. Period.'
M.K.I.

The solution is straightforward. Let go of your red cars. Let go of resisting the experiences in life that you've been conditioned not to want. Let go of being attached to different things happening instead. Be clear on what you want and take action towards it, while surrendering to all that life brings. Let life happen in all of its weird and wonderful ways. Be willing to experience all of life, not just some of it. Take this invitation to wake up from your conditioning and calmly coexist *with* life.

If by now you can see the value in living conflict-free, then you'll be glad to hear that I've observed it is much easier when engaging each moment with self-awareness...

 TIP *For more support and free resources to apply the principles of Calm Cure to CONFLICT, visit my Calm Clan: www.calmclan.com/conflict*

Chapter 2

AWARENESS

The Heart of Healing

Self-awareness is the term I use for being aware of the aspect of your *self* that is *aware*. What do I mean by this statement? Inside you, right now, there is an awareness that is aware of this moment happening, including for instance, the words you are currently reading. Yes, your mind is reading, but your awareness is aware of the words on the page. See the difference? Some call this awareness the 'observer', the 'witness', the 'stillness' or the 'being'. It really doesn't matter what we label it. What matters most is that we are aware of its presence within us and make it a priority to experientially engage life with self-awareness from now on.

> *'What you are looking for is what is looking.'*
> ST FRANCIS OF ASSISI

AWARE OF THE FULL SPECTRUM

Awareness is aware of all of your inner thoughts, emotions and physical sensations, along with your external events and experiences. Awareness is still, silent, spacious, peace-filled presence; it is not otherworldly, but as real as you can get. It is the most permanent and unchanging aspect of you, so I would go as far as to say it is *who* you really are. Silently observing the happening of *every* inner and outer experience that you've ever encountered. There has never been a moment in your life when this awareness has not been present within you, even if you haven't always been aware of its presence. Awareness is aware of the full spectrum of life and by being self-aware you can find it is possible to coexist calmly with anything that comes your way.

The safe haven of awareness

In the same way that the sky doesn't care what flies through it, awareness is not concerned with what it is aware of. Irrespective of how 'good' or 'bad' life appears to be on the surface, your underlying awareness remains still, calm and well – always.

One of the core reasons why we tend to recoil from experiencing the full spectrum of life is that we've tried to do so without self-awareness. We've been taught to think *about* life, rather than directly experience it from the safe haven of our permanently present and peaceful awareness. Thinking about life gets us caught up in a world of thoughts and, if they happen to be negative, then that is how we feel. However, by being self-aware – aware of the aspect of your self that is aware – you can experience the unconditional calm of your awareness, instead of *only* the ups and downs of your conditioned mind.

Without self-awareness, our thoughts *about* what's happening determine our experience of, and relationship *with* life. But here lies the problem with relying solely on this non-aware thought-based perspective on life: The mind makes sense of reality by judging if it is good or bad, right or wrong, better or worse, or positive or negative. If based upon our preconditioned mind-made judgements, life appears to be bad, wrong, worse or negative, then the habitual tendency is to resist the perceived problem and experience the negative side effects of our resistance to 'what is', including anger, anxiety, sadness, fear, guilt, grief, shame, frustration, loneliness... the list goes on. But as already mentioned, your awareness is an ever-present ongoing state of still, silent, spacious calm within which you can comfortably coexist with all of life – free from the countless symptoms of conditioned conflict.

Self-awareness sits at the heart of healing.
Being self-aware is not a way of avoiding or
escaping life, but the way to have a healthy
relationship with life so that you can experience
the full spectrum without suffering.

BEING SELF-AWARE WITH GAAWO

Let's engage self-awareness now with a technique that I call 'GAAWO', an acronym for 'Gently Alert Attention Wide Open', which is a remarkably easy way to still your thinking mind and coexist with life by being self-aware. Although GAAWO is simple, the analytical mind can interfere with it, so I recommend that you adhere to the following three golden rules – not just the first time, but every time you use GAAWO:

Rule 1: Play with GAAWO

When you were a child you played. You were curious, explored and didn't give up at the first hurdle. Growing into adulthood, we often forget how to play and get caught in the trap of trying to get it right first time. We can lose interest or give up, if we don't get the results we want or aren't immediately perfect at it. We can talk ourselves out of things before we even begin! For the best results, play with GAAWO. Follow the instructions, see what happens, jump higher than any judgements about it not working and keep GAAWO-ing until it's second nature.

Rule 2: Don't think about GAAWO

You cannot think yourself into GAAWO for it to work. If you are thinking about it then you will be in your mind and end up one step removed from the experience of self-awareness. Without the experience, you will quickly come to the conclusion that the technique doesn't work. It does. So be aware of the difference between thinking about GAAWO and engaging it.

Rule 3: You can never do GAAWO later

One common mind trap is the subtle planning to do it later. You can accidentally think about how you really should engage GAAWO, or that you will do so after the conversation or once you've found a solution to your problem, for example. You can do GAAWO anytime and anywhere and if you don't, there's a high chance you are postponing the benefits. Why wait, when you can be calm now? Are you happy with the rules? Let's get GAAWO-ing!

HOW TO ENGAGE GAAWO

Look ahead at this page and, as you continue to read the words on the page, relax your gaze to let your field of vision spread out to the left and right. Do not look directly at anything to your left and right. Instead, use your peripheral vision simply to notice what is there. What you can see may be blurred and not in sharp focus; that's OK. Your intention right now is gently to let your attention open up wide to the left and right as you continue to gaze ahead at the words on the page.

Now notice what it is like to let your gaze open up wider, both upwards and downwards, again without looking up and down. In your peripheral vision you might be able to see your lap and the colour of the clothes you are wearing. Above you might see the ground beyond the book and/or the wall as it extends upwards to meet the ceiling, if you're inside somewhere. Irrespective of where you are or what you can see, just gently let your attention open up more widely to notice both above and below, simultaneously.

Continuing to gaze ahead, now notice what it is like to let your attention open up wide to the left and right and above and below so that you are gently alert with your attention wide open. What's happening in your mind? Is it chaotically busy or calmer and quieter than before engaging GAAWO? Has your inner experience of this moment become more restful? Are you thinking about the past or the future, or are you present noticing the here and now? Can you become aware of an inner spaciousness or even stillness, as you engage GAAWO now?

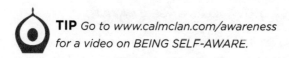

TIP *Go to www.calmclan.com/awareness for a video on BEING SELF-AWARE.*

THE POWER OF PRESENT-MOMENT AWARENESS

Every step of Calm Cure involves engaging self-awareness with the GAAWO technique. (If you know other ways to engage awareness, such as the Ishaya Ascension Meditation, which I also teach, then engage the stillness or silence when using Calm Cure.) Being self-aware enables you to access the healing power of awareness and be at peace with life.

> *With GAAWO you disengage your conditioned mind and are able to experience life unconditionally in a calm and comfortable way.*

Fully experiencing the complete spectrum of life requires you to be present, in the here and now. Did you know that there are no present-moment thoughts? All of your thoughts are *about* the past and future. Even thoughts relating to now are about a past moment because the thing has to have already happened for the mind to be able to commentate on it. Most people are so preoccupied by their thoughts *about* life that they miss the peace, purity and potential of the present-moment experience. One step removed from reality, they are distracted by their mind-made stories and feeling their thinking. Self-awareness is therefore your doorway to the 'inner peace that's always present', and is required to engage freely whatever life is presenting. By being self-aware, you go beyond the dramas dredged up by a mind that is set on incessantly judging life, and are able truly to heal. By heal I don't only mean fixing, changing or improving your mind, body or life circumstances, but by experiencing life from the perspective of the awareness within you that has never had a problem with anything that's happened in the 'now', ever.

> *Resistance melts away as you align*
> *with the light of your awareness.*

Rising above resistance involves engaging present-moment awareness whenever you realize that you're caught up in your thinking mind. In a recent Harvard University study, it was found that the average person is 'lost in their thinking mind' for 47 per cent of the day.[1] That's half of every day and ultimately half a lifetime, so be vigilant. The average person is missing the present-moment reality by meandering around in their illusionary mind-made versions of life. Don't be average. Be awesome and experience your precious gift of life – by engaging GAAWO and hanging out in self-awareness. It is a wonderful way to live fully and be liberated from the common stresses and struggles that so many of us frequently face.

THE 'PEACE WITH' STRATEGY

Can you see how limited and conflicted life inevitably becomes, if it is *only* allowed to show up how you think it should? Calm Cure is focused on cultivating 'peace with' the full gamut of life. As we've covered, it is focused on healing your conflict with life, as that is the hidden cause of many physical conditions, emotional issues or persistent life problems. With self-awareness you aren't as negatively affected by your conditioned judgements, resistances and attachments, and are able to live in harmony with anything that has been causing you concern. If you're willing to entertain this possibility, then you will see value in using a technique like Calm Cure, which clears conflict-based conditioning for the cultivation of a steadfast peace with life. To be super-clear on the differences between the 'fix it' and the Calm Cure 'peace with' perspective, here is a summary of the differing perspectives involved:

'Fix it' perspective	'Peace with' perspective
There's something wrong with my life and me.	There's ultimately nothing wrong with life or awareness.
I need to fix, change and improve myself and my life.	I want a healthy relationship with myself and my life.
Problems are anything that is wrong, bad, worse or negative.	Problems are anything that I've been conditioned to resist.
Negative emotions, stress and suffering are due to what happens.	Resistance to 'what is' causes negative emotions, stress and suffering.
I need to take action to fix the problem so that it goes away.	I need first to get 'peace with' the life experience.
Life will improve if I push away the bad things and work hard to get what I want.	Life will improve when I'm not in conflict and say 'bring it on' to the life I've got.
Problems happen in life and I need to do everything I possibly can to avoid them.	Life is inviting me to be a more self-aware and unconditionally loving presence in the world.

Despite there being clear differences between the perspectives, let me be clear. I'm not saying that you should become passive and not take action to improve your health, life or world. We can be and do whatever we want, and it's fun to be creative, go for inspiring goals and help to make the world a *better* place. However, what I am saying is that we can't be free until we are willing to engage life in all its forms.

Also, sometimes engaging a 'fix-it' strategy can prove helpful and Calm Cure honours this by helping you to have a positive mindset towards life, so that you don't feel the need to resist. It also clears the blocks to being proactive and creating more desirable outcomes. By adopting the 'peace with' perspective, you will learn how to achieve this from a foundation of calm instead of conflict. You will treat a core cause of countless problems by healing the hidden belief that something is wrong with you and your life.

Possessing the 'peace with' perspective heals your relationship with reality and stops you seeing any benefit in battling life.

The positive purpose of problems

Problems are whatever we have been conditioned to think are wrong and reject. They therefore highlight where we are living in a conditioned and limited way. By accepting this possibility, we start to view problems as invitations to see where we've been living in fear instead of love and not letting life show up in all its weird and wonderful ways. With this kind of attitude, perceived problems become the perfect route to learning how to love and live fully and freely. Through self-awareness and developing the willingness to experience all of life, not just some of it, life is able to teach us how to be a more unconditionally loving and positive presence in the world.

 TIP *For more support and free resources to apply the principles of Calm Cure to be SELF-AWARE, visit my Calm Clan: www.calmclan.com/awareness*

SUMMARY: BE CONFLICT-FREE

Before learning the Calm Cure technique, here is a summary of the first two chapters:

- Life happens on a spectrum of possibilities – sometimes you get what you think you want and sometimes not.

- Health and happiness are the result of having a willingness to experience everything that comes your way during daily life.

- Problems are anything that you've been conditioned to resist because of attachments to experiencing something else.

- What you are in conflict with, you remain connected to.

- When you bring conscious calm to unconscious conflict, the body can heal and you stop creating the same life problems over and over again.

- To calm conflict, you need to reduce reactive resistance and ascend beyond unseen attachments.

- Anytime you have a problem, there are three parts at play:

  1. Problem name
  2. Symptoms
  3. Conflict experience

- The conflict experience is any life experience that you don't want and therefore reactively resist.

- You can discover your conflict experience by exploring the inner experience of the condition or life problem.

- The awareness that is aware of your condition or problem is still, silent, spacious, peace-filled presence.

- Being self-aware using GAAWO is the starting point to coexisting calmly with life.

- The common approach is to fix, change and improve whereas the Calm Cure aims to first get 'peace with' life.

- Problems highlight where in your life you are living in fear and limitation instead of love and freedom.

- With Calm Cure, you are going to clarify your conflict experiences and get 'peace with' all aspects of life.

- When you are consistently self-aware with an unshakable peace with life, you are free from the unconscious conditioning that is causing you to live in a conflicted way.

Chapter 3

THE CALM CURE TECHNIQUE

I've had the pleasure and privilege of working with thousands of individuals through my clinics, public events and academy courses. Over the years I've created a number of techniques that have gone on to be included in 10 books, shared on countless conference stages, used by practitioners working in a wide range of fields and featured on radio and television in multiple continents. I never set out for any of this to happen. Just with a burning desire to help as many people as possible not to suffer their way through life, as I did before learning what I now pass on. In 2007, I accidentally created the Mind Detox method while working on a health detox retreat in Spain. Mind Detox went on to be included in my book, *Heal the Hidden Cause*, and shown on three hit television series. It is a very powerful therapeutic technique for resolving the past events negatively impacting us today.

After observing the need in my clients and myself for both therapy and meditation, I trained and graduated as an Ishaya Ascension teacher in 2009 after meditating day and night for several months. In 2012 I then created Mind Calm followed by the Body Calm technique a couple years later. Mind Calm aims to prove that the secret to success is stillness and helps us to move from stress and serenity by getting 'peace with mind'. Body Calm gives the body the rest it needs to recover and brings about the holistic harmony required for better health.

*It lights me up to know that someone somewhere is
benefiting from using these techniques every day.*

OVERVIEW OF THE CALM CURE TECHNIQUE

Calm Cure is inspired by my previous techniques and offers a systematic way to apply my 'peace with life' philosophy to heal the root-cause conflicts negatively impacting us in daily life. If you are struggling with something then it is common to be told to 'accept it', 'let it go' or 'surrender', yet many find it hard to do so because they've been conditioned to do the exact opposite. When you are willing to experience both ends of the spectrum of life possibilities and everything in between, your conflict collapses. Calm Cure is therefore a way to transcend your conditioning to be conflicted and be free from all kinds of problems. The technique consists of three steps:

1. **Clarify the Conflict:** Clarifies the conflict experience, including what you are resisting and attached to.

2. **Calmly Coexisting:** Focuses on calmly coexisting with the conflict experience and determines how at peace you are with both experiences showing up in your life and the presenting condition/problem.

3. Calm the Conflict: Changes your attitudes towards life so the conflict is no longer justified.

SIX SUCCESS STRATEGIES FOR THE BEST RESULTS

Although Calm Cure is simple, used correctly it can deliver remarkable results. Before using the technique, I recommend reading and digesting the following six success strategies to avoid the common pitfalls and achieve the best results:

1. Be innocent

People using my methods have often used other techniques and been disappointed when they haven't been successful. Irrespective of what's happened in the past, leave it where it belongs and step forwards with optimism. Suspend judgement and jump in with as much childlike curiosity as you can muster. Leave doubt at the door and don't let scepticism stand in the way of your success.

2. Recognize covert resistance

One of the first resistances you may need to recognize and resolve often relates to the technique itself. You possibly haven't wanted to 'go there' and the mind can throw up covert resistances that aren't always recognized as such. You can find yourself comparing, judging and criticizing the technique, engaging 'poor me' thoughts or getting distracted by external stuff when using the technique. Covert resistance can be right under your nose and consists of subtle ways not to engage the technique and do what's being asked. For example, 'This technique is a load of rubbish and isn't going to help me.' 'It is so unfair that I have to go through this.' 'I think I should wait until I have less stuff going on in my life.' 'I'm not any good at things like this so there's no point even trying.' Be vigilant of the thoughts and feelings that are preventing you from fully engaging the process. They can often be subtle ways of avoiding, which is a symptom of resistance.

3. Be super-gentle

Reading a book and using a technique like this can make you more aware of certain habits that may be negatively impacting your health, relationships and overall life. But what's very important to remember is that, although your life *is* your responsibility, you have not intentionally done it to yourself and it's not your fault. Blaming yourself is just a form of resistance and a distraction that postpones peace, restricts the body's ability to heal and life's ability to bring you something new. The past need not dictate your future. Now is the only moment that matters. Choose a new way of being and doing now, and be super-gentle on yourself as you proceed.

4. Stay out of your story

Thinking and analysing is commonly used to comprehend intellectually. However, this is not what Calm Cure is designed for. When progressing through the technique you want to notice any times you are in your head thinking. When thinking, you are one step removed from the experience and 'feeling your thinking' instead. This stops you from accessing the power of awareness, which is what is going to do the majority of the healing work.

Feel your way through the steps with little internal dialogue. If it is ever hard, uncomfortable or appears not to be working, notice if you are thinking more than experiencing, then continue with present-moment awareness by using GAAWO.

5. Keep your eye on the ball

The purpose of Calm Cure is to cultivate an inner willingness for anything to happen in your external life. The technique begins by asking how the condition/problem makes you feel. Emotions can help you find where you've felt the same way, so that you can discover the *experience* that you are in *conflict* with, i.e. the conflict experience. When first using Calm Cure it is common to focus on trying to get peace with the emotions you are feeling *because* of what's happening, such as hurt, scared, frustrated, etc. It is vital to remember:

> *Emotions are a reflection of your relationship with life. Negative emotions are commonly the result of resistance and attachment.*

Do not use the technique on 'negative' emotions. Use Calm Cure to get peace with what is happening that is making you feel a similar way to how the condition/problem makes you feel. The 'negative' emotions will automatically go when there is no resistance and attachment. Keep your eye on the purpose of the technique – to get peace with what's happening and not emotions – and you will find it is easier and works much better.

6. Commit to persist until you succeed

Do you really want to experience a healthier relationship with your life? Are you willing to keep going until you get the results you want? People who've had complete remissions from illnesses or transformed their life for the better have made it a high priority in their life, for as long as it has taken. I didn't do it all in a day and I continue to go beyond my conditioning when I see something I haven't seen before. Be careful not to just 'try' it a couple times or throw it away if you have a bad day or hit a bump on your journey. Everything that you've been successful at has taken time, commitment and perseverance. You may need to practise the Calm Cure to get good at it and bring about the inner attitudinal shift required to heal your body and see changes reflected in your life. Decide now not to quit and to persist until you succeed.

When using Calm Cure, keep these success strategies in mind and, before moving on to learn the Calm Cure technique, make sure you understand the principle shared in the first two chapters. Reread them again if necessary. If you still have questions then ask me, or my team of Calmologists, by contacting us through my Calm Clan Community on Facebook. If you *are* ready and willing to calm your conflicts towards life, then the wait is over.

Next up I share the instructions for the Calm Cure technique plus a list of the most common conflicts. Then in Part II we will apply the Calm Cure to key areas of life that can be negatively impacted by conditioned conflict, including health, emotions, relationships, career, money, time and the wider world.

THE CALM CURE TECHNIQUE

Decide what you want to get peace with using Calm Cure.

This can be a physical condition or life problem you are finding challenging. Then engage GAAWO (*see Chapter 2, page 21*) and do the following:

Step 1. Clarify the Conflict

This step clarifies the conflict experience including what you are resisting and what you are attached to.

- How does the condition/problem make me feel?

Describe your inner experience of the condition/problem in one to five words and/or phrases. For example, frustrated, weak, limited, unable to cope, restricted, alone, confused, under attack, helpless, irritated, drained, trapped, vulnerable, etc. Note that these words and phrases are not the problem name or physical/ life symptoms, but how it feels to have the condition/problem.

- Where in my life have I felt this way?

Recall a life event or circumstance when you felt the same way as how the condition/problem is making you feel. When working on a physical issue, don't answer with the physical symptoms/ condition, e.g. 'My back pain is making me feel restricted.' Instead, look for an external life event/circumstance during which you felt the same as to how the condition is making you feel. For example, if feeling unable to cope, then where in your life have you felt that way? Or if feeling restricted, where have you experienced restriction?

'I've been feeling unable to cope at work' or 'I'm feeling restricted in my relationship'. For life problems, the life event/circumstance may or may not be the problematic situation you are working on, so it may be earlier in your life.

- **What is happening that I do not want?**

Clarify your root-cause resistance – what's happening that you don't want and are resisting the most. Remember, negative emotions are symptoms too, so don't answer with an emotion – such as frustrated or hurt – but with what is going on that's making you feel the way you do. 'I'm feeling unable to cope at work because of the intense workload,' or 'I'm feeling restricted in my relationship because I have no time for myself.' In these cases, the root-cause resistance would be the 'intense workload' and 'no time for myself'. By removing the resistance to what is happening in your life, you will no longer feel unable to cope or restricted, for example. Aim to state your root-cause resistance in one word or short phrase.

- **What would I rather be experiencing instead?**

For the above examples, you would probably much rather be experiencing a 'manageable workload' or 'time for myself'. If you have been rejected, would you much rather be accepted? If you have been experiencing being unsupported, would you rather be supported? This final question of step 1 provides your attachment and when combined with the root-cause resistance is the conflict experience. Aim to state your attachment in one word or short phrase. Move on to step 2 when you have clarified your resistance and attachment.

Step 2. Calm Coexisting
This step focuses on calmly coexisting with the conflict experience and determines how at peace you are with both experiences showing up in your life and the condition/problem.

- Think or say: All things are possible and I am willing to experience [*state the attachment*] sometimes and I am willing to experience [*state the resistance*] sometimes.

- Rest into the willingness for both possibilities to coexist calmly within you and to sometimes show up in your life.

Allow 15–60 seconds to do this and notice how your inner experience changes, as you hold the intention to be willing to allow both possibilities. Remember, you are using Calm Cure because you want to calm the conflict and be at peace with life. Don't wait for the willingness to arise like magic, but instead actively choose to be willing now because you know it is the most empowered and free way to be.

- On a scale of 0–10, with 10 being very high, how would I rate my willingness for both life experiences to happen?

If you rate below 10/10, go to step 3.

- On a scale of 0–10, with 10 being very high, how would I rate my peace with experiencing the condition/problem?

If you rate below 10/10, go to step 3.

When you rate 10/10 for both of the above questions, you have successfully calmed the conflict.

Step 3. Calm the Conflict
This step is not compulsory if, having clarified the conflict in step 1, you can calmly coexist with it in step 2. If not, then the following step changes your attitudes towards life so any remaining conflict is no longer justified.

Calm Past

- Recall a memory of a symbolic event when the root-cause resistance has shown up in your life.

If your root-cause resistance was 'confused' then it would be a memory when you had lots of confusion going on. Trust that the first relevant memory that comes to mind is the right one.

- What can I know now, that if I had known in the past, I would never have resisted the event in the first place?

List three to five things that you wish you had known then, which would have helped you to be more at peace with what happened.

- Where do I feel these knowings within my body?

Imagine the movie of the memory, but this time looking through the eyes of the 'younger you' with the knowing(s) in that area of your body. Allow 30–60 seconds to do this.

- On a scale of 10–0 with 0 being 'the resistance is gone and I am at peace with it now', how would I rate the memory? If 0/10, repeat step 2. If above 0/10, do Calm Future.

Calm Future

- Is it possible for me to be at peace with experiencing the root-cause resistance at some point in my life?

If your root-cause resistance is 'confused', then consider if it is possible for you to be at peace with being confused at some point in your life. You would not be using Calm Cure if you didn't hope that it was possible so the answer is usually 'yes'.

- What will the 'future me' know, to be at peace with it then?

- Where do I feel these knowing(s) within my body?

- Recall a memory of a symbolic event when the experience of the root-cause resistance(s) has shown up in your life.

It may be the same memory as used in Calm Past, or a different one. Imagine the movie of the memory, but this time looking through the eyes of the 'older you' with the knowings in that area of your body. Allow 30–60 seconds to do this.

- On a scale of 10–0 with 0 being 'the resistance is gone and I am at peace with it now', how would I rate the memory? If 0/10, repeat step 2.

If you rate above 0/10, then return to step 1 to re-clarify the conflict, as you need to use the Calm Cure on a different conflicted experience.

See Appendix I (pages 151–52) for an at-a-glance version of the Calm Cure technique.

COMMON CONFLICT EXPERIENCES

Here is a guide to common resistances and attachments. If any of them resonate with you, i.e. you know that you resist one side and are attached to the other, then use Calm Cure. When possible, come up with your own words/phrases. For example, the attachment may be to being *loved* but the resistance may be to something other than being *judged*. Note that these conflict experiences are not emotion-based, but life happenings that it is common for us to end up conditioned to be in conflict with. Imagine how free you would be if you had no conflict with anything on this list.

Resistance	Attachment
Judged	Loved
Unwanted	Wanted
Unsupported	Supported
Rejected	Accepted
Ignored	Noticed
Unheard	Heard
Unappreciated	Appreciated
Unrewarded	Rewarded
Criticized	Complimented
Misunderstood	Understood
Excluded	Included
Wrong	Right
Confusion	Clarity
Uncertainty	Certainty
Not good enough	Good enough
No control	In control
No time for myself	Time for myself
Limited options	Lots of options
Being on my own	Having people around
Don't know what to do	Know what to do
Not get my own way	Get my own way
Unable to do what I want	Able to do what I want

TIP *For more support and free resources to apply the principles of Calm Cure, visit my Calm Clan: www.calmclan.com/calmcuretechnique*

Part II

CALM CURE
YOUR LIFE

Chapter 4

HEALTH

Helpless to Healed

Over one billion prescriptions have been given out in England each year since 2014. Incredibly, this is few in comparison to the USA, which currently leads the way as the most prevalent user of prescribed drugs, consuming 75 per cent of all pharmaceuticals, despite only making up 5 per cent of the world's population. Millions of people are heavily reliant on drugs, which is regrettably unsurprising due to what we've been conditioned to believe about health and healing. Growing up, at the early signs of sickness I would be taken to the doctor's surgery to be given a diagnosis and pick up a prescription. Sound familiar? The consequence of this conditioning is an unhealthy dependency on doctors and a helplessness to heal without popping pharmaceuticals.

I became interested in holistic health in my twenties when I started using Mind Detox to help people to resolve the mind-based causes of physical conditions. And now, well over a decade on, I've seen so many people heal by resolving the mind-based causes that I'm convinced the potential exists within almost anyone to heal. As long as they explore why the body has created certain physical symptoms and do the inner work required to resolve the possible root-cause reasons. Saying this, I'm not suggesting that all conditions are 'mind-caused' or that you should never call upon doctors or use drugs ever again. Rather, that if you want to heal a specific condition or stay fit and healthy, then it is wise to adopt an integrative strategy that includes medical advances alongside principles and practices like Calm Cure that take account of the scientifically proven mind–body connection.

STOP TREATING SYMPTOMS

Medical professionals, taught by classical institutions, are often trained to view the body as separate from the mind and focus on finding physical reasons for physical conditions. Diagnoses are generally given based upon the collection of symptoms showing up within the body. If you have swelling, stiffness and pain in your joints, then it's *because* you've got arthritis. If you have tiredness and weight gain then it's *because* your thyroid may not be working properly. Or if you have abdominal pain, bloating, cramping and/or undesirable bowel habits, it is *because* you've developed irritable bowel syndrome (IBS), which is commonly said to be caused by food intolerances or stress. Although it sounds like these medical labels are providing diagnoses as to *why* you have the condition, upon examination, these explanations are not diagnosing the cause, only offering a medical name for your group of symptoms or diagnosing symptoms of other symptoms, with the real root-cause(s) remaining unknown.

Look beyond medical labels to explore the root-cause reason because there is a big difference between receiving a diagnosis and defining the underlying cause.

When working with clients with physical conditions, I will usually begin by asking what diagnosis they have received from their doctor. Then, having been given the medical name for the condition, I will enquire what they were told is causing their issue, with the answers usually including age, 'wear and tear', 'because it just happens' or 'bad luck'. For me, these answers don't satisfy my curiosity when wanting to understand *why*. Taking the above examples further, being informed that you have painful joints *because* you have arthritis is not being told the cause; it is only being given a name for your symptoms. Or receiving the diagnoses of a thyroid condition as the cause of your weight gain, or IBS due to food intolerances, also falls short. Why has the thyroid stopped functioning or why has the body become intolerant to certain foods? When you get the answers to these questions, you move much closer to finding and resolving the cause, which is often a conflict experience.

Physical condition
Condition **name**
Physical **symptoms**
Conflict **experience**

Stress is also a symptom

Those open to alternative approaches to improving health often conclude that stress is the cause of their conditions. Stress has been linked with inflammation, reduced immunity, cardiovascular disease, digestion disorders, and the speed, growth and spreading of certain cancers. Through my own research into the subject, I've found hundreds of medical journals linking stress with a vast array of health conditions. Based upon the evidence, chronic stress is most definitely harmful to health. However, I don't believe that stress is the ultimate cause of conditions, but rather another one of the many symptoms, brought on by a lesser-known cause.

Stress is not caused by stress. Stress is the consequence of something other than itself. This means stress is a symptom too, but of what? Yes, you guessed it – conflict. Remember, although it appears on the surface that you are stressed because of what's happening, stress is not caused by circumstance, but by your relationship *with* what occurs. By calming conflict, we have a better relationship with life, and experience less harmful forms of stress and a calm physical climate that promotes anti-ageing and optimum health.

Learning to listen to your body

Seeing the link between health and your relationship with life is vital. It takes much of the mystery (and misery) out of illness and proactively places the power to help your body heal in your own hands. This move from feeling helpless to being healed includes the skill to remain calm and know how to interpret what your body is communicating through the conditions it creates. Until you develop this ability, it's easy to feel like a victim of your body and inevitably need to rely on externally sought diagnoses and drugs. You wouldn't be reading this book if that's what you wanted, so keep reading within the context of a condition if you have one. You can gain clarity on the conflicts that you may need to calm to help your physical form return to full fitness.

What is your body saying via your physical conditions?

Offering real-time feedback, the body is a brilliant barometer as to how in harmony with life you are. You therefore want to view physical conditions and their associated symptoms as red flags: highlighting where any conflict may be happening. Then use Calm Cure (*see Chapter 3, page 35*) to explore the underlying causes and resolve them. To do this, the first step of the technique asks:

- How does the condition make me feel?

- Where in my life have I felt this way?

- What is happening that I do not want?

These three questions take you on a journey from tuning in to the inner experience of the condition to discovering the life event/ circumstance when you've felt that way and clarifying the thing you are resisting the most, which is your root-cause resistance.

Let's say you've been diagnosed with arthritis, for example, so you may respond to these questions: 'The arthritis makes me feel incapable. I've felt that way as far back as I can remember due to the strict parenting I received. Ultimately I feel incapable because of the constant criticizing I received growing up.'

With this recognition, your root-cause resistance – the life experience that you are resisting the most – would be towards 'being criticized'. If you would much rather be experiencing 'being praised', for instance, then you would have found your conflict experience. To help your arthritis heal, you would use the rest of the Calm Cure to be willing sometimes to be criticized (resistance) and sometimes to be praised (attachment). By calming the conflict, you would feel far less incapable, be much freer to do what you want without fear of being criticized, and see improvements in the symptoms, if they were being caused by that individual conflict experience.

Meet Mary, who had chronic knee pain

I met a Mary at a public talk in London. She had been off work for weeks, was reliant on a walking stick and said nothing she'd done to heal her knee had worked, which was also making her feel demoralized. When asked, 'How does the knee problem make you feel?' she answered: 'I can't support myself and fear that I'm getting old.' Immediately, she realized that she had just described how she had been feeling during the months before the onset of the knee problem. I then worked with her to get peace with her conflict experience of 'not being able to support herself'. Within minutes she reported that the pain 'wasn't there!' and that her knee felt strong enough to support her weight without her stick.

In the case of headaches (condition name) your symptoms would most likely be pain in the head. When clarifying the conflict, you might respond to the questions by saying, 'The headaches make me feel like I'm under attack. I've been feeling this way at work because my boss is a bully and, ultimately, I hate being told what to do.' In this case, the root-cause resistance would be 'being told what to do' and the attachment would be something along the lines of 'doing what I want'. As before, you would use the rest of the Calm Cure technique to become willing to experience being told what to do sometimes and being able to do what you want sometimes.

Remember, Calm Cure is all about clearing the conflict on your side of the metaphorical fence, so that you no longer resist life when it doesn't show up how you would like. By doing so, you naturally feel better and are free from 'negative' external forces. Your boss may continue to act in a similar way, but it won't bother you any more and if it serves for you to stand up to them, then you will be able to do so in a calmer and confident way.

Clarifying the conflict experience

Getting clear on the conflict experience is the foundation to the rest of the technique. If you don't clarify the conflict experience correctly, then you won't be working on the right thing. You can then find it harder to recall the best past event(s) to use (step 3 of the Calm Cure technique) and the conflict causing your condition may continue.

How does the condition make me feel?

When asking this, it helps to substitute 'condition' with the name you have been given so it is more personalized: psoriasis or fatigue, for example. Then tune in to how it feels and trust the first words that come to mind to describe it. Avoid overthinking it, by instead focusing on what it is like within you; to be living with the condition and/or symptoms. At first some people can find it tricky to do this because we are so used to focusing on the diagnosis or symptoms. But the truth is you *already* know the inner experience of the condition very well, but like many of us, can miss what is right under your nose. It is almost like the way you feel has become the wallpaper of your daily life, which you no longer notice. Keep it simple: you are describing how it *currently* feels, within you, to have the conditions and symptoms, so you don't need to look into the past to try to remember. It is how it feels, right now.

Meet Cristina, who had nausea

When asked about how the nausea made her feel, Cristina said, 'I feel like I'm going to puke!' This answer just gave me a physical symptom, so I replied, 'I appreciate that, but how does feeling like you are going to puke make you feel?' To which she said, 'It's frustrating because I can't do what I want today.' This provided the experience that she was resisting, i.e. not being able to do what she wanted – which we discovered was actually how she had been feeling for a couple of days before the nausea started. Her attachment was simply 'doing what I want' so we focused on helping her calm that conflict.

We used Calm Past (in step 3) and her 'antidote knowing' was 'everything gets done eventually so I can just relax'. After installing it into the past memory, we tested the work using Calm Coexisting (step 2) and she was now 'willing to experience being able to do what I wanted sometimes and not being able to do what I wanted sometimes'. Within five minutes, the nausea had gone.

Use words that best describe what the condition feels like to experience. For example, under pressure, irritated, restricted, weak, incapable, invaded, helpless, alone, out of control, etc. Notice that these words are not the names that you've been given for the condition. They are also not physical symptoms, such as itchy or painful. They are *describing* words for how it feels, within you, to be experiencing the symptoms and condition. You will be amazed by how such a simple question – 'How does the condition make me feel?' – can reveal so much and how quickly you can uncover the potential hidden cause.

 **TIP** *Go to www.calmclan.com/health for a SELF-HEALING guided meditation.*

CALM CURE YOUR BODY

Ready to use the Calm Cure on a condition? Decide upon something you wish to help heal with the technique and then turn to the instructions in Chapter 3 (*see page 35*) and give it a go. Having done so you should experience peace *with* the conflict experience and with the condition itself. I recommend using the Calm Cure in a similar way to taking a prescription. You wouldn't take one pill and give up if healing didn't occur instantly. You may need to use the Calm Cure a few times on the same condition to make the shift required to create the inner climate necessary for your return to full health. This may include digging deeper to find a few conflict experiences.

USING THE CONDITIONS DIRECTORY

Starting on page 156, you will also find a Conditions Directory listing the common mind-based causes of 101 physical conditions. For each condition, you will find a list of common causes along with their recommended 'Calm Cure Thought' for cultivating a healthier attitude towards life. If you are struggling to clarify your conflict experience, or would like additional guidance on what might be causing your condition, then use this directory alongside Calm Cure.

The directory is based upon my observations during years of clinical practice and my investigations into how the body speaks to the mind. In addition, I've trained hundreds of practitioners in my methods and so have had the unique opportunity to read thousands of case studies submitted by students taking my academy courses. Combining all this data, I've seen trends in the common mind-based causes of many conditions. By sharing them with you, I hope they help you to discover what your body may be saying through the conditions it has created.

To use the directory, find the condition that you are curious about, read through the list of common causes and feel which one(s) resonate with you the most. If you find a potential cause, ask: *On a scale of 0–10, with 10 being very high, how would I rate my resistance to having this experience?* If you rate it 7/10 or above then it is worthwhile using the Calm Cure technique to calm your conflict.

For example, if you have a cough, then you will see the mind-based causes include: Feeling unseen and/or unheard, unable to ask for what you want or need, and inaction. Let's say you resonate most with 'feeling unseen'. That would be your root-cause resistance so you would pick up the Calm Cure at the question: *Where in my life have I felt this way?*, and continue with the rest of the technique from there.

HOW I USED THE CALM DIRECTORY ON MY KIDNEY STONE

While writing *Calm Cure*, I ended up in hospital in Mexico needing an operation to remove a kidney stone. It had stopped my right kidney from working and the pain was immense. In short, it was a medical emergency. I was glad to receive the doctor's diagnosis and surrender to the necessary surgery, and was grateful for the effectiveness of the medication which reduced the pain over the following days.

Once the emergency had passed, I explored the possible mind-based causes of kidney stones in the Calm Directory. From the list, 'fear-based anger and needing to be hard to protect' resonated with me so I used the Calm Cure to resolve it. I found I was resistant to being 'bullied and rejected' and attached to being 'loved and welcomed'. After calming the unconscious conflict I felt a profound inner gentleness and connectedness. So it turned out that I needed a kidney stone to soften my heart and be able to love more fully and freely!

Incidentally, this experience also highlighted the belief that, due to the work I do, it wasn't okay for me to ever have any sort of physical issue. Recognizing this has enabled me to embrace my humanness and be even more open to the full spectrum of life.

HARMONY HEALS AND LOVE IS THE INNER HEALER

I invite you not to use the Calm Cure with the sole purpose of healing your body. Instead, use it with the *soul* purpose of cultivating your willingness to engage with the full spectrum of life. This will help you to love life in a much more unconditional way, i.e. without conflict and with an openness to experience whatever happens. Loving life does not prevent you from being proactive about making changes. You just engage change from a foundation of love and freedom rather than fear and conflict. The ultimate healer within you is love. Clear the conflict that has been preventing you from loving all aspects of yourself or life and you can heal the unhealable, due to the calming harmony that occurs within your heart, mind, body, soul and circumstances.

The body heals when the fire of unconditional love burns up your conditioned conflict.

 TIP *For more support and free resources to apply the principles of Calm Cure to your HEALTH, visit my Calm Clan: www.calmclan.com/health*

Chapter 5

EMOTIONS

Upset to Upbeat

Humans have inhabited this planet for around 200,000 years. Yet despite the passing of so many generations, many of us still find it hard to live with a major component of being human: namely our emotions. Similar to life, emotions are happening, however much we may wish we could flick a switch and turn them off at times. Emotions are an intrinsic and inevitable part of the human experience. Each day, we experience a spectrum of feelings, some comfortable and others less so.

How you relate to your own mind and life plays a major role in the emotions you experience most often. The more you get 'lost in your thinking mind' and you are in conflict with life, the more 'negative' emotions you will end up feeling. At the same time, many of us have also been conditioned to have an unhealthy relationship *with* our emotions, which is a core cause of much stress, struggle and suffering.

Raised by adults unwilling to experience the full array of their own emotions, they would resist witnessing us expressing our feelings so fully and freely. As children we may have been encouraged to tone down or turn away from the intense ones that were perceived to be problematic. Based upon the misinformed assumption that some emotions are 'positive' and others 'negative', it is common to be conditioned to attempt to avoid the 'bad' ones at all cost. This conditioning has led to millions of us fearing certain emotions, habitually resisting and controlling them and engaged in a fight with our feelings.

> *Emotional freedom doesn't come from fixing, changing or improving emotions, but by having peace with all emotions.*

For emotions, the goal of Calm Cure is not only to experience the ones that we've been conditioned to believe are 'positive'. That would involve being attached to one end of the emotional spectrum and resistant to the other. The 'peace with' approach focuses on cultivating the ability to coexist calmly with *any* energy. All the flavours of the emotional kaleidoscope can serve in highly beneficial ways when they are befriended, felt fully – with no conflict – and used with clarity and purpose.

EMOTIONAL FREEDOM

Peace *with* emotions is incredibly liberating. Just think how free you would be if you weren't worried about how life might make you feel. How free you would be if you weren't scared of standing out or being seen, not resistant to the possibility of people criticizing you, or perhaps not succeeding at your first attempt. If we aren't going for grandiose goals, it is often because we are held back, not by circumstance, but by a fear of how life might make us feel. Imagine what would happen if you were willing to experience *any* emotion. You would be free to be and do anything! With Calm Cure, we engage a two-part strategy for enjoying true emotional freedom:

1. Clear resistance towards certain life circumstances because you naturally don't experience the emotions caused by conflict.

2. Cultivate a willingness to experience the full spectrum of emotions because some energy that you've been conditioned to resist is actually rising up to help you to heal and create.

Using Calm Cure for peace *with* life, you naturally experience far fewer 'negative' emotions due to the absence of conflict. Also, instead of controlling your emotions, so that you only experience certain ones, you feel them fully without losing your *self* in the process. This is possible by being self-aware – attentive to the aspect of your self that is aware – while emotions move through you. This removes the stress and suffering that appears to be caused by how you feel.

Emotions become problematic when you are in conflict with them. You've been taught that some are 'bad' and anytime you notice them happening, your conditioning wants them gone. However, it is not the emotions, but your resistance that makes them so unpleasant and causes them to stick around longer than necessary. When you don't judge or resist their existence, due to an attachment to feeling something else, they aren't so uncomfortable and are allowed to arise and subside without you having to do anything to 'fix' them. In fact, you see that it was your attempts to improve them that were preventing them from moving on.

'But I hate feeling bad! Surely the negative emotions have to go away so I can feel good again?' With self-awareness and the 'peace with' approach, you can get to a point where you stop caring so much about how you happen to be feeling and live liberated without working so hard to keep your mind happy. Trust me, life is much freer and more fun when you are not so fixated on how you are feeling all the time. To make the shift from upset to upbeat – irrespective of what emotions are happening – here are four principles you need to know:

Principle 1: You are not your emotions

What emotion are you currently feeling? Has there ever been a time in your life when this emotion was not present? What has been present the entire time? You know you have emotions because you are aware of them and there has also been a time in your life when the current emotion has not been happening. Anything temporary cannot be *you*. You are the permanent aspect of your self that doesn't come and go. So what's the most permanent aspect of you? Awareness. Knowing this naturally changes your relationship *with* emotions. If they are not you, then you can learn to take them less personally. You don't need to fight with or fear your feelings because you are not the transiting energy passing through, but the vast sky of still awareness that all emotions temporarily exist within.

You are the awareness that is aware of your emotions.
Although you have emotions, you are not your emotions.

Principle 2: External life is not the cause of all emotions

'I'm sad because of my childhood', 'I'm hurt by what she said', 'I'm anxious because my future is uncertain'. Though it appears 'negative' emotions are due to what happens, it is not necessarily the case. We feel hurt if we think about and are in conflict with, what a person said or did. Anxiety is not the result of an uncertain future, but because we are thinking in a conflicted way about the future, i.e. are resistant to certain things happening and attached to specific outcomes. Emotions are the result of your relationship with what's happened, is happening now or might happen. Stop judging negatively and reactively resisting, and you may find 'negative' emotions have a magical way of evaporating into nothing.

No person, event or thing has the inherent power to make you feel any which way. When you accept that external life isn't the ultimate cause of your 'negative' emotions – but rather conflicted thinking *about* life is – you stop being a victim to circumstance. You also save lots of time, money and effort trying to fix, change and improve your circumstances in order to feel better. Repeat after me:

'I'm feeling what I'm feeling because
I'm thinking what I'm thinking.'

TOP TIP: TREATING TRAUMA

It is worth acknowledging that there are occasions when it appears significant past trauma is causing present emotions, especially when we aren't aware of any thinking going on. Despite this, it is highly beneficial to entertain the possibility that you can heal the trauma by clearing the unconscious conflict. If you do so, you may find that this principle stands true and the past events are not the ultimate cause of the current emotions, but rather more subtle levels of thinking have been. If you are in any doubt about working on trauma without a trained professional, please seek support.

Principle 3: Peace is not the absence of emotions

Emotions don't need to disappear for you to experience peace. I've consistently had intense energy in my solar plexus area. Yet despite the presence of emotional energy – that my mind would label as 'negative' – I am experiencing peace with it because I'm hanging out in self-awareness. This is possible because the awareness that is aware of all emotions is already and always peace-filled. Awareness remains calm despite transiting temporary energy. If you are waiting for your emotions to stop so that you can experience a numb void of emotionless peace, then the good news is that your emotions don't need to go anywhere for you to enjoy consistent calm.

Emotions have happened every day of your life so far. There is a very big chance that they will do so for the foreseeable future. Don't wait. Peace is not the absence of emotions. Peace is what the awareness that is aware of your emotions feels like. In other words, being self-aware, you can experience a sense of inner stillness *alongside* any temporary emotion. To discover this remarkable reality for yourself, engage GAAWO now and notice that if you aren't thinking by remaining present and aware, you will be experiencing a quiet presence of peace *and* whatever emotion is currently passing through. It is not either/or it is *both* calm and emotions.

Awareness is aware of your emotions. Awareness is always peaceful. Therefore, peace is aware of your emotions.

Principle 4: You do not want to be emotionless

Emotions are energy *in motion*. Without energy you're a goner and with it you are highly likely going to be a go-getter. As long as you are unwilling to experience the full spectrum of emotions, you will be suppressing your vitality. For optimum health you need energy and as far as the body is concerned, all energy is good. Emotions don't harm the body; it is conflict towards them and life that does. Therefore, to resist your emotions is to limit the energy that the body needs to heal and be healthy.

Everything you want in your external life is also made up of energy and requires energy to create. So to improve your life, you really don't want to be emotionless. Far from it; the more emotional energy, the better. Aim to achieve 'peace with' your emotions by being self-aware. Notice when you're thinking about how you are feeling or resisting your emotions (this is easy to recognize because there will be suffering going on). Then engage self-awareness with the help of GAAWO. It is also beneficial to become conscious of your breathing, as the breath tends to become restricted whenever we don't want to feel fully. Letting the emotional energy be present within you, with no resistance, allows the power of your emotions to rise up and their positive purpose be actualized.

 **TIP** *Go to www.calmclan.com/emotions for an EMOTIONAL FREEDOM guided meditation.*

CALM CURE ON COMMON EMOTIONAL ISSUES

These principles provide the perfect platform for using the Calm Cure technique (*see Chapter 3, page 35*). If you resist certain emotions ('good' or 'bad'), then your intention is not to make the 'bad' emotions go away, but to coexist calmly with them. Saying that, when it comes to using the Calm Cure technique on emotions, you won't aim to sometimes feel sad and sometimes feel happy, for example. Instead, you will apply the technique to heal the hidden conflicts that are causing you to relate to life in a way that is justifying the 'negative' emotions. Remember, anger, sadness, fear, guilt, grief and all other 'negative' emotions are a consequence of resistance and attachment. By adopting the two-pronged approach of being willing to feel your feelings *and* calming the conflict that is causing 'negative' emotions, you completely transform your relationship *with* any emotions that you've had a problem with.

> *Make the shift from frustration and fear*
> *to emotional freedom.*

Most people I meet are suffering with the same emotions, which I refer to as the 'famous five' – anger, sadness, fear, guilt and hurt. For any of the ones that are most relevant to you, if you find a common cause that resonates with you (from the lists provided), use the Calm Cure on it. Let's say, when reading about anger, you resonate with the common causes of 'lost and confused'. Use the technique to explore where in your life you've felt that way and continue from there. Below I also share my recommended 'Calm Cure Thoughts' – which you are invited to think whenever you remember to do so throughout your day (or during your daily Calm Meditation Sittings – see resources for how to learn Calm Meditation within my Calm Clan). They can help to cultivate a healthier attitude towards your emotions and life.

Anger – including frustration and irritation

Anger is a secondary emotion, meaning you don't feel angry unless the primary emotions of hurt, sad or scared are present. Anger is often a protective mechanism used to push away what has made you feel hurt, sad or scared. Anger usually requires resistance brought on by the belief that things *should* happen *your* way. When healing anger, don't let the frustrated feelings distract you from the underlying primary emotions. To use Calm Cure on the causes of anger, explore how else the person, event or thing made you feel. When you resolve the source of the hurt, sadness or fear, then there will be no justification to be angry any more. You may continue not to agree with whatever has happened, but you will be at peace *with* it and more effectively take the action that is required.

The upside of anger

Bursts of anger or frustration can be very helpful for saying what needs to be said or doing what needs to be done. Just as engaging anger with self-awareness can dramatically alter your inner experience of it, to the point where it feels more like passion or love. It is when anger is chronic that it often becomes counterproductive.

Common causes

Hurt, sad, scared, vulnerable, invaded, violated, alone, lost, confused, unprotected, unsafe, pushing away to protect, perceived lack of love, support and/or security, 'It's not right/fair'.

Calm Cure Thought

I am safe, surrendered and say 'bring it on' to life.

Sadness – including depression and feeling low

Sadness is commonly a result of thinking patterns based on the themes of lack, limitation, victimhood, comparison, unfairness, wrongness or 'poor me', although it may appear that you are sad *because* of circumstances. You feel what you are thinking about. If you are engaging a cynical mind-set with depressing thoughts, then that is how you will feel. Use Calm Cure on whatever you are feeling compelled to think negatively about.

To cultivate happiness, heal the habit of negative thinking by intentionally looking for what is present and right, instead of focusing on what's missing or wrong. If you are feeling sad, you might not feel like you can do what I'm suggesting, but don't wait to feel better before taking action. Even the smallest of steps now can make a big difference to your long-term happiness.

The power of praise

Praise heals the belief that there is something wrong with you and your life. Finding things to praise rather than criticize is the foundational first step in developing an attitude of gratitude. With the power of praise, what you were sad about doesn't need to change for you to feel better. You can immediately lift your mood and begin your journey back to joy... starting now!

Common causes

Resistance to the past, something needs to be better/different, powerlessness, pointlessness, focusing on what's wrong, over-comparison, feeling unseen, perceived lack, lacking compelling purpose, resisting certain emotions to the point of numbness. 'I wish it had not happened that way', 'What's the point?' 'Life is difficult' or 'life is unfair' thinking.

Calm Cure Thought

I am grateful for the good in life and feel lucky to be alive.

Fear – including scared, apprehensive and anxious

Fear requires you to forget how powerful and resourceful you actually are. By ignoring the fact that you have survived every event or circumstance that has happened during your lifetime. Fear also feeds off your unwillingness to fully feel it. In fact, it is your resistance to feeling scared that gives it power to limit or control you. The moment you are willing to feel it, fear can be used as a positive and powerful force for good. Don't worry, you won't end up paralysed by fear, if you allow yourself to consciously feel it. It is resistance to feeling it that gives fear powers to limit your life. Allowing feelings of fear to be present within you can provide the strength you need to heal and face whatever life brings.

The force of fear

Let go of the conditioned labels of 'fear' or 'anxiety' and be open to relating to these energies as your inner power. Having had what I thought was fear and anxiety for years I discovered, when I allowed it the freedom to rise up within me, that the energy was a potent inner power. I had been unintentionally suppressed my inner power because I believed the feelings were bad. Breathe deep, feel it fully with self-awareness, and you may also find it is a potent and powerful force for good.

Common causes

Vulnerable, no control, unprotected, unloved, 'The world is a dangerous place', 'I'm not safe', 'I'm going to get into trouble', 'my inner strength can hurt others', scared of own power, 'I'm unsupported', 'something bad might happen'.

Calm Cure Thought

I am powerful and possess all I need to be safe and to succeed.

Guilt – including regret, remorse, blame and shame

Guilt is commonly caused by inner conflict consisting of a resistance to what you've done (or not done) and an ongoing attachment to needing to have acted differently. Guilt feels justified because we believe holding on to it helps us not to make the same *mistakes* again in the future. However this is not the case. Guilt is harmful to health and keeps us connected to the past. Remember, whatever you resist persists, so the unconscious focus on not doing it again increases the likelihood of you repeating the same actions.

The guidance of guilt

When healing guilt, regret, remorse, self-blame or shame, be willing to forgive the 'younger you' for not knowing better. You shouldn't have known better because you couldn't have known better because you hadn't yet learned what you know now. Acknowledge that given the same circumstances today you would not do the same as you did in the past. Have faith in your older and wiser present-day self who now knows better.

Common causes

Fear of repeating past mistakes, resisting past decision(s), self-punishment, attached to things happening differently, being hard on yourself, self-critical, attachment to being a good person, 'I should have known better', 'I'm a bad person'.

Calm Cure Thought

I am forgiven and free, always doing my best.

Hurt – including offended, emotionally wounded and upset

Nobody has the power to hurt us emotionally. This is because you don't feel hurt because of what someone's said or done, even if everyone in the world would agree it was horrible or wrong. Hurt is caused by what you are doing on your side of the fence, inside your own mind. You feel hurt when you *feel your thinking* about what's been said or done. It can be incredibly freeing to recognize that nobody has the power to hurt you. That anytime you are hurt you have accidentally given your power away by thinking about a past moment. By being self-aware you can observe the habit of hurt-based thinking and stop getting so caught up in the hurtful story.

The holding of hurt

Do you want to be right or do you want to be free? Choose to let go of holding on to hurt and instead be an unconditionally loving force for good in this world. If someone has acted in a 'hurtful' way, rise above the mental stories by being willing to see them in a compassionate way. With compassion, you don't get down in the hole to suffer with the other person. Instead, you remain in the calm of self-awareness that doesn't take anything personally. It also helps to remember that everyone would choose to experience peace and love – if they could make the conscious choice rather than react due to their conditioning. If someone doesn't know how to be peaceful, loving or happy yet, they need your compassion, not criticism.

Common causes

Vulnerable, powerless to the impact of other people's words and/ or actions, no control, unable to get what you think you need, resistance to the past, playing the victim, unloved, rejected, abandoned, unwanted, lack of compassion.

Calm Cure Thought

I see the innocent desire for peace and love within everyone.

ENLIGHTENED EMOTIONAL FREEDOM

Let's end this chapter with an invitation to raise the bar into an enlightened relationship with emotions. Have you noticed that it requires a subtle 'checking out' of the present-moment reality to know how you are feeling? For you to know that you are happy or sad, anxious or frustrated, involves engaging in some form of mental activity, i.e. by asking: *What am I feeling?* and then attaching a mind-based label to the energy. When 'lost in the thinking mind' your attention leaves the present-moment reality to focus instead on thoughts about the past.

> *Emotions are remnants of the past. Shadows of how your conditioned mind was made to feel a few moments ago.*

Emotional energy may be within you now. But it exists because of something that happened in your mind a few moments ago. By being self-aware with *all* of your focus on *this* moment, you can be aware that you are feeling something, but without the conditioned mental constructs of 'positive' or 'negative'. This higher-level attentiveness to what life is presenting now makes you far less interested in or concerned about the temporary emotions passing through. You stop being so fixated on your feelings and therefore don't have to manage and control them. There is also less resistance and attachment to life happening any particular way because you aren't attempting to make and keep your mind happy.

How am I feeling?
I don't know, I don't care and I absolutely love my life.

Don't forget, the only part of you that cares about how you are feeling is your conditioned mind and you are reading this book because you want to live free from conditioning. An enlightened relationship with your emotions comes from being so filled up by *this moment* that you don't care how your mind feels about the past or future. With practice it won't matter how you feel and when that happens you are emotionally free.

 TIP *For more support and free resources to apply the principles of Calm Cure to your EMOTIONS, visit my Calm Clan: www.calmclan.com/emotions*

Chapter 6

RELATIONSHIPS

Conflict to Connection

Over seven billion people currently live on planet Earth. As recently as the 1930s there were three billion. You don't have to be a mathematician to see the simple fact that there are now a lot more people in the world to cohabit peacefully with than ever before. But despite the potential implications of growing population numbers, what's most important is the relationship you have *with* your self, your nearest and dearest, and the spectrum of souls who happen to cross your path each day.

One of the main reasons why relationships are such a tricky landscape to navigate lovingly is that there aren't ever two people on Earth who are exactly the same and would agree on absolutely everything. With different upbringings, cultures, beliefs, values, habits, preferences, opinions and even gods – we may live in the same planet, but collectively, we see, hear, feel and experience over seven billion different worlds.

We are not meant to agree on absolutely everything and others should not be and do what you think they should. Everyone is born free to have a unique experience of life.

How on earth can we all get along? Using Calm Cure you can clear any conditioned conflicts so that you can move towards being more perfectly loving instead of trying to make people morph into your ideas of perfect. By love, I'm referring to the only love that really exists: unconditional love. Most of the people I meet (including myself) struggle at times to love all parts of themselves and that is why they find it so hard to love others too. They are entangled in a conditional form of mind-based love that consists of judgements, requirements and hoops that need to be jumped through, either by themselves or others, so that they are deemed loveable. This isn't love. It's just one big performance, including a pile of masks, mistaken meanings and a disconnection from the truth.

RELATIONSHIP REFLECTIONS

Your relationships with others are a perfect reflection of your relationship *with* yourself. As long as you are in conflict with who you currently are, you will project that outwards and find the same conflicts showing up in your external relationships too. Meaning if you are resisting your present incarnation, due to attachments to some ideal idea of the person you think you *should* be, you will remain separate from love. Furthermore, if you are waiting for your mind to decide that you are loveable, then you will also end up waiting a very long time. Remember, your mind uses judgement to make sense of reality, so there is a high probability that you may never satisfy its criteria for love. To love unconditionally, you therefore need to get to know and be in harmony with the full spectrum of yourself and others, which again is possible with the power of self-awareness.

Calming inner conflicts creates connected relationships.

CALM GAME: LOVEABILITY LIST

Write a list of all the things that you believe need to be fixed, changed and/or improved about yourself so that you can be completely loveable. Your list may include the shape, weight, wellness, etc. of your body, personality traits – being funnier, cleverer, less moody, etc. – as well as external stuff such as the achievement of certain goals, or anything else that you think needs to be better so that you are loveable. This list is an important one to write because everything listed are the conditions that you are placing upon your loveability.

With your list you have two options:

The first option is to engage the 'fix it, change it, improve it' strategy with the aim of satisfying all of the conditions. This may or may not be possible, but one thing for sure is it will take time. There's also a chance your mind will move the goalposts at some point, by adding new items to the list because it can only think *about* love, but the mind cannot experience it directly. This leads to it assuming more needs to be done before you are deemed loveable.

The second option includes calming the conditioned conflicts sitting in your way of loving unconditionally and discovering the inner source of love. This option takes no time, involves zero effort and requires nothing to change before self-love is possible.

I certainly know the option that I prefer!

LOVE WITHOUT AWARENESS BECOMES FEAR

Love without awareness is reliant on the analytical mind and inevitably ends up conditional. The mind cannot comprehend 'unconditional', because it uses reason and check boxes. All of the conditions that determine whether someone is loveable or not, are based upon the past, and what you've been conditioned to believe is loveable and what is not. Love from the mind usually includes a silent 'because' along with some kind of performance-related justification: 'I love you because... [*you are good-looking/ nice to me/popular, you agree with me*],' for example. Love without awareness is problematic for so many because if we aren't self-aware, we will be inclined to experience a false love with its foundations in fear and conflict.

Fear can arise when you are not connecting from awareness.

Being self-aware you naturally discover that your awareness is an unconditional, all-allowing, all-encompassing, all-embracing, enduring presence of love. Amazingly, you can find that the presence of your inner being *is* love. Or in other words, at your core, you are the love that you've been seeking from external means. This enables you to *live in love*, engaging everyone with attentiveness upon the *inner* being of love that you are. Until I discovered this, 'I love you' had become a question – 'I love you?' – I would graspingly ask to check that I was loved by hearing the words back. If there was ever a slight pause and the 'I love you too' didn't return as fast as a boomerang on speed, I would freak out. 'What's wrong?' 'Are we OK?' 'What can I do?' 'Why don't you just love me as I am?' 'I'm a good person, you know!' My fear and resultant insecurity, neediness and jealousy ruined a series of perfectly good relationships.

The problems with performance-related love

Growing up, many of us are rewarded with love and reprimanded with its removal. At the nursery I went to as a kid, if I did something wrong I had to stand and face the corner. Perhaps your penalty was the naughty step, being sent to your room, a disapproving look or a slap somewhere? This conditioning causes many of us to feel the need to start performing to get love from our parents, partners and peers, even strangers in the street! Being unaware of the unconditionally loving presence of your own awareness, you inevitably end up forced to look for, and trying to get, love from outside yourself, either by finding your perfect match or by ensuring everyone who crosses your path loves you. If the source of love is outside, it can be taken away and performance-love kicks in almost immediately.

Performance-love makes us puppets on the strings of fear.

Living with the fear of love being taken away leads to unhealthy relationship habits like dependency, jealousy, oversensitivity, neediness, ownership, arguments and loneliness. Again, at the heart of these fear-based behaviours is conflict. Including resistance to love being taken away and attachment to love being attained from every external source possible. It is a recipe for disaster due to the necessity to twist and contort yourself in order to be loved by others, along with the pressure it puts on the people you are trying to take love from. It is also a lost cause because you are trying to get love from places where it can't be found. Yes, people may love you, but you won't feel it or fully accept that they do. Frustration, distrust, closing down, distancing, unworthiness, self-dislike and unresolved hurts all end up standing in your way of connecting deeply with yourself and others.

However, once you find that the love you are looking for is inside, you find there is nothing to fear and these habits can finally fall away. Relationships are given space to breathe, grow, and move on if needed, and you get to love freely with an open palm. You get to be free and single. You get to be free and in a committed relationship. You get to be free because you've moved from conflict to true connection.

> *'Relationships are not here to make you happy or fulfilled... they are here to make you conscious.'*
> ECKHART TOLLE

Clean up your side of the fence

For the best relationships, look to be self-aware and heal any conflict happening within you, instead of trying to fix, change or improve other people so that they are loveable. It is easy to fall into the trap of making relationship conflicts about the other person. What they said or didn't say. What they did or didn't do. What they meant or didn't mean. But to be proactive about moving from conflict to connection, you'll need to focus on cleaning up your side of the fence. It is not anyone else's job to make you happy, it is yours. How you feel is down to your relationship *with* the particular relationship, which is a perfect reflection of your relationship with yourself.

Lots of 'relationships' mentioned then, but the only relationship that I would recommend focusing on healing is the one with your self. Whatever you are feeling in relation to someone else is caused by what's happening inside you, so that's where to look to resolve any issue. When you heal the inner conflict, what the other person does or doesn't do won't be a problem any more. You won't take it so personally when you know your perceived lack of love has nothing to do with anyone else.

TOP TIP: WHEN LEAVING IS A LOVING ACT

The caveat to this approach is if there is any form of abuse going on. On these occasions, it's time to call it a day and get the hell out of dodge. It's not your job to fix the other person or make them stop their destructive relationship patterns. It is their responsibility to wake up and resolve their inner conflict. If this sounds harsh, it is quite the opposite. Walking away can be the very wake-up call they need to heal the stuff that's preventing them from experiencing real love. If you stay, you can limit them from the lessons they need. If you find it hard to leave, then clear the conflict within you that would cause you to stay in an abusive relationship.

WHAT LIMITS LOVE?

Let's turn our attention to cleaning up our side of the fence. Conflict-based relationships are less loving, due to the conditioning that eats away at the heart of them. I've observed over 20 symptoms of conflict-based relationships that limit love – many of which I've done myself! I share them with you now, not so you can beat yourself up or immediately break up, but so that you can determine if any of them are playing out in your relationships. Until you are aware of them, you can't do anything to resolve them. But by shining a light on these limiters of love, the benefit of engaging self-awareness and using Calm Cure to clear any conflicts standing between you and love-based connections becomes obvious.

Read the following descriptions to find the relevant one(s). Then answer the clarity question and (if appropriate) use the Calm Cure technique (*see Chapter 3, page 35*) to resolve the conflict that's causing you to behave that way. For example, reading the list you might see that you've been judging that your partner works too late for your liking. Using Calm Cure, you would ask: *How does my partner working late make me feel?* If it makes you feel 'unwanted' then you would use the rest of the technique to get peace with it once and for all.

Love limiters

Conditioning: Your beliefs about relationships: how people should act, how they should look, etc. Conflict arises when you don't accept that your beliefs are going to be different and/or if you try to force your beliefs upon someone else. Ask: *What do I*

believe the other person should be/do and how does it make me
feel when they are not how I think they should be?

Expecting: Expectations are often not openly expressed and the other person is left oblivious. Nonetheless, you then make it their fault for failing to meet *your* expectations. Conflict occurs when your expectations aren't met. Ask: *What expectations do I have that are not being met and how does it make me feel when I don't get what I expect?*

Judging: You judge the other person as bad, wrong, worse or negative. Conflict arises due to resistance to the 'bad' and an attachment to the person being different or better. Ask: *How does the person being* [insert judgement] *make me feel?*

Comparing: You compare your relationship with past partners, other friends or family members, your ideas about how loved ones should be, or couples who appear to be more in love or happier. Conflict arises when some other relationship appears to be better. Ask: *What comparisons am I making and how does it make me feel when other relationships appear to be better?*

Assuming: Assuming other people see the world the same as you and should therefore act the same way too. You also assume that they know what you want or that you know what they want. Conflict kicks in when assumptions are not accurate and/or not met, e.g. 'I thought you'd buy me a bottle of water, if you were buying one for yourself.' Ask: *How does it feel when my assumptions are not met?*

Mind-reading: Attempting accurately to predict what someone else is thinking, why they did what they did, what their actions mean, e.g. 'The kids prefer Dad because they went to the shops with him instead of staying home with me.' Ask: *What mind read am I making and how does it make me feel?*

Taking: Engaging relationships with a 'what's in it for me' attitude. If you are taking, you end up in conflict due to inevitably being let down at some point. It's also a performance-based relationship, which is not love-based. Ask: *What do I believe is lacking within me that I need to take from others, and how does it make me feel to lack it?*

Counting: Linked with taking, this is when you do nice things but keep a tally, e.g. 'I did x for you and you've not...' Conflict occurs if you don't get back in equal measure to 'your giving'. You're not giving if you are doing so to get something back. Ask: *How does it feel not to get back in equal measure?*

Perfecting: Trying to achieve your idea of 'the perfect relationship'. Snoring and difficult days aren't permitted, for example. Conflict occurs when life doesn't fit your ideas of perfect. Ask: *What do I think is imperfect about the relationship and how does it make me feel not to have a perfect relationship?*

Controlling: When you try to control the other person so that they are how *you* think they should be. This shows up in covert ways: undermining comments, emotional manipulation, ordering the other person about or withholding affection, etc. Conflict occurs when they don't do what *you* want. Ask: *How am I controlling and how does it feel when I don't get what I want?*

Blaming: Condemning others causes 'hard-hearted', conflicted relationships, e.g. 'If you had booked a table then we would have been able to eat here.' Instead of being 'in it together', the focus is on finding fault. Ask: *Where does blame show up in my relationship and how does it make me feel to blame the other person and/or be blamed?*

Guilt-tripping: Intentionally making someone feel bad is a way of manipulating future behaviour, e.g. 'Why didn't you call me when you knew it was a big deal for me?' This is not love but guilt-tripping to get your own way. Ask: *How am I trying to make the other person feel guilty and how does it feel to do so?*

Trap-setting: When you test the other person's love by setting traps for them to fall into. Like not telling them that you've had your hair done or pointing out a new outfit or saying how your day went – to see if they ask or make a comment. It is trap-setting if you intentionally hold back to see if they notice. Ask: *What is going on within me that makes me feel the need to set traps?*

Competing: Winning points, being right, or getting one over the other person. The relationship is about competition, not connection, e.g. 'I was right and you were wrong' or 'I told you so'. You lose, if you don't want both to win at having a great relationship. Ask: *What feelings are driving my need to win?*

Withdrawing: Pulling back, closing down and giving the cold shoulder or silent treatment, e.g. 'What I feel isn't important so there's no point saying anything.' Withdrawing can be a punishment towards others or be used as a strategy to make the other person give attention and engage you. Ask: *How am I feeling, within me, when I need to withdraw or close down?*

Protecting: Having been hurt in the past your focus is on avoiding future hurt and therefore you hold back from connecting fully. You have a wall up, are unwilling to be vulnerable and/or don't let anyone close. Ask: *What happened that makes me protect myself and how does it make me feel?*

Defining: Placing limiting definitions upon yourself and/or others, e.g. 'I'm the type of person who… [*is always clean/on time, doesn't want to have sex that often, etc.*].' Conflict arises when you are resistant and/or attached to the definitions you've made about yourself/others. Ask: *How does it feel when I'm asked to be or do things outside the remit of my definitions?*

Generalizing: When you make sweeping statements about the other person, e.g. 'You always do x, you never do y.' Ask: *What sweeping statements do I make about the other person and what does the way I think they always are make me feel?*

Personalizing: Making the other people's thoughts, feelings and actions about you and taking things way too personally. Their stuff is their stuff. Yours is yours. Ask: *What am I taking personally about the other person and how does it feel, within me, when I do?*

Analysing: When you excessively analyse everything that's said or done. The relationship becomes very 'heady' with lots of thinking and little heart connection, to the point you are thinking *about* the relationship more than you are relating. Ask: *What am I overanalysing, how does it make me feel?*

Contradicting: Aiming to find ways to hold the opposite opinion or challenge what's said or done. Usually due to an unwillingness to connect and with a desire to break rapport, even though you really want to get on, find agreement, connect and feel understood. Ask: *What am I resisting or attached to that is causing me constantly to contradict?*

Undermining: When you either privately or publicly put down the other person. Usually with jibes, talking over, degrading digs, moaning or bitching behind their back and/or by making slanderous statements. Ask: *Who am I undermining, and what feelings are going on, within me, that cause me to do so?*

Saving: When the relationship is based upon saving the other person or you are focused on fixing them. These types of dysfunctional dynamics are based upon the other person's brokenness and your efforts to rescue them. Ask: *How do I feel when I see someone that I think needs saving?*

Not prioritizing: Not giving time and making other things more important than love. You keep working when the other person wants a hug or take the relationship for granted and don't invest time or effort in nurturing it. Ask: *What am I making more important than love and why?*

Not committing: Being half-in the relationship. Love ends up limited because your lack of commitment creates doubt, constant questioning if it's right, testing of the relationship, holding back until you're sure etc. Ask: *How does it make me feel when I consider fully committing to this relationship?*

LOVE WITHOUT LIMITS

I appreciate this is a rather long list of love limiters. Remember; when you are self-aware, many of these habits naturally fall away. However, you may have found a few that show up regularly in your relationships. If this is the case, then I recommend using Calm Cure along with the following six top tips for moving from conflict to connection.

1. Be the person you want to love

People try to take from others what they don't experience within themselves. If you are of the opinion that someone else should be kinder, communicative, giving, etc., then ask: *Where can I be more of what I want?* When you become the person that you want other people to be, many conflicts dissolve away because you don't resist the lack of certain attributes in others and aren't attached to them being what you think you need.

2. Take everything as an invitation to love better

We often want other people to change so we don't have to. However, as the saying goes, when you point the finger there are always three pointing back at you. You are the common denominator in all of your relationships. Look for themes in your arguments, disappointments and common feedback you receive from others. Don't waste time playing the blame game. Assume any issue you have with someone else is an invitation to learn how to love in a more unconditional way.

3. Give, give and give some more, especially praise

Service sits at the heart of the most successful relationships so ask: *How can I serve you?* as opposed to *How can I get what I think I need?* When a problem arises in a relationship, find ways to give and be of service. When you make the relationship about how you can help the other person be happy, feel loved and have a great day (without trying to fix or change them), then it's amazing how fluid and fun relationships become.

CALM GAME: THE 5:1 RULE

Giving praise is a powerful way to transform any relationship and connect on a deeper level. Find things to appreciate and praise about others. By choosing to praise instead of criticize, it brings out the best in others and makes you feel great too.

As a general rule, aim for a 5:1 ratio by giving five praises to one criticism. It leads to others being more open to hearing if there is something they could benefit from improving and you can also arrive at a point where you don't see things wrong with the relationship.

Play with it, be genuine and have fun!

4. Stop 'should-ing' all over the relationship

'He should be more A and less B or she shouldn't have said X or done Y.' So many conflicts stem from 'should-ing'. Notice when you think someone else should think, feel or do what *you* think they should. Drop all of the shoulds and you *should* find it results in more loving, kind and supportive relationships.

5. Be willing to share more of yourself

Raising defensive walls within relationships is common. We are conditioned to hide our true feelings in an attempt to avoid getting hurt or being seen as weak. There is great strength in vulnerability. It takes courage to let your 'weaknesses' be seen. I am amazed by how quickly conflict evaporates when one party is willing to share honestly what's really going on for them, e.g. 'When you did that I felt scared that you might leave me,' or 'When you work late, I question if it's because you don't want to be home with me.' It's very hard to be in conflict with someone waving the transparent flag of vulnerability.

> *The more of yourself you share and let be seen, the more other people have to love about you.*

6. Don't go changing, trying to please me

Would you feel loved by someone if they always wanted you to be different? How loved would you feel if you had to live with a constant pressure to perform and a desire for you to be someone different to who you naturally are? My Spiritual Teacher once asked, 'Are you willing to commit fully to this relationship, even if the other person never changes?' Well, are you? Forcing others to meet your conditioned requirements for what's 'loveable' only leads to a fake love that has foundations based in conflict. Freedom comes from loving without limits.

TIP *Go to www.calmclan.com/relationships for a CONFLICT-TO-CONNECTION guided meditation.*

CALM CURE COMMON RELATIONSHIP ISSUES

These love limiters and recommendations are relevant to any relationship type, including life partners, friends, relatives, colleagues and even people you've never met, such as celebrities or politicians who may be bothering you. They clarify common causes of disconnection and disharmony, which can be resolved with Calm Cure. The technique can also work wonders on these three key relationship issues:

Eternally single: For singletons seeking love, focus on clearing any conflict that could prevent you from meeting that special someone. If you are resistant to being single then you will most likely remain that way. Or if you are attached to meeting your 'one and only' then fear-based *neediness* tends to push away what you want. Also, if you are holding on to unresolved hurt from past relationships or underlying fear of intimacy, then again you want to do the inner work so that you are open to allowing people close. Explore: *How does being single (or the thought of being in a relationship) make me feel?* Clarify the inner experience and bring calm to any conflict.

Broken heart: Use Calm Cure to get peace with relationship break-up(s) and move on feeling whole and complete. Explore: *How does the relationship break-up make me feel?* Let me assure you, it is not the relationship ending that's making you feel bad, but your conflict with it ending that is. Resolve your root-cause resistances and get peace with it being over to be free to love, wholeheartedly, again.

Let's talk about sex: Sex is a hot topic in many relationships. Highlighting much conditioning that's coming between couples and preventing them from enjoying what is a beautiful way to connect, be fully seen, vulnerable, celebrate love and have fun. For many, sex has become nothing more than a habitual physical act or a way to let off some steam, while for others it can be used to pacify a lack of inner love or low self-esteem. Those raised with religion can be taught that sex is a sin outside of marriage or if it's not to conceive, often causing guilt or shame. Explore: *Beyond the physical sensations, how does sex make me feel?* Use Calm Cure to heal your relationship with this sacred and sublime act so that you can enjoy a healthy and happy sex life.

 TIP *For more in-depth articles on the above three issues, visit my main website: www.sandynewbigging.com/relationships*

Meet Sarah, who was having problems in her sex life

Sarah was having heated arguments with her partner over their sex life because they only 'did it when he wanted to'. She would have emotional outbursts anytime she 'made a move' and he didn't want to have sex. When asked how it made her feel she said, 'Panic, powerlessness, used and tossed aside.' Exploring where she'd felt that way, she recalled an ex-boyfriend who chased her for weeks and then didn't contact her after finally 'bedding her'. She explained that it was the first time anyone had ever left her and she felt anxious and helpless not to be the one in control.

Using step 2 of Calm Cure, she rated 5/10 for her willingness to be in control sometimes and not be in control sometimes. We used the Calm Past and her knowings were: 'I actually knew he wasn't right for me but I got together with him because I liked the attention' and 'other boyfriends have said I am a great lover'. Testing the memory, she still felt there was a resistance of 3/10 towards what happened.

Lastly, we used Calm Future and she said, 'The "future me" is clear that she wants a relationship based upon love and freedom, and not fear and control, and the "future me" knows that she doesn't need sex to take love because she is the love that she used to look for outside.' After installing these knowings, she felt at complete peace with sometimes being in control and sometimes not. After using Calm Cure, Sarah reported that the emotional outbursts and neediness had gone. If he didn't feel like it sometimes then she would cuddle instead and the lack of 'issues' around sex had made it more fun, leading to him wanting it more often.

NO REASON NOT TO LOVE

Loving unconditionally requires you to be self-aware and present. When present you are fully focused on *relating* rather than being in your mind thinking about the *relationship*; one step removed from the living experience of love. Aim to give all of your attention to the person you are with. Relationships offer a wonderful opportunity to go beyond mind-based conditioning and wake up to conscious connections. Commit to connecting fully and freely by clearing conditioned conflict, and you will inevitably run out of reasons *not* to love. When this happens, you discover the home of oneness-infused peace, love and happiness has always been in your own heart.

TIP *For more support and free resources to apply the principles of Calm Cure to your RELATIONSHIPS, visit my Calm Clan: www.calmclan.com/relationships*

Chapter 7

CAREER

Average to Awesome

According to the Conference Board Job Satisfaction survey, under half of the US population (48.3 per cent) are satisfied with their jobs.[2] Whereas in the UK, an Investors in People survey reported that an even higher 60 per cent of the population are not happy in their work.[3] Based upon official employment figures, with the USA sitting at around 150 million employed and the UK at around 30 million employed, it means there is potentially a massive 90 million people across the USA and UK who are unhappy with their current career.[4-5] Imagine how high the number might reach for the *world* population. This career dissatisfaction epidemic is again largely due to our conditioning to be in conflict, which negatively impacts how we relate to our work. I wish I could send a memo to the millions of people around the world who are unhappy in their jobs, informing them that it's possible to wake up to a wonderful work-life, and how Calm Cure can help!

I measure the ideal career situation by three basic standards:

1. You work because you choose to.

2. You feel satisfied by the work you do.

3. You earn more than you need.

Modest standards, yes, but due to the collective conditioning surrounding 'work', I've observed few people satisfy all three. If you were to be surveyed today, how would you rate your career, based upon the above criteria? If you feel forced to work, dislike what you do or feel disappointingly rewarded, then keep reading. My hope is that you go beyond wishing your weekdays away – to get to the weekend – and you never experience the sinking 'Sunday-night feeling'. You can love what you do so much that the lines between work and pleasure fade away and the day of the week becomes irrelevant. I've achieved this myself, not by working harder to change my external career circumstances, but by attuning to a healthier attitude *with* the work that I do.

> *Satisfaction is not the result of what you do, but*
> *your relationship with what you do.*

SERVICE WITH A SMILE

Whether you are seeking employment, starting out or established as self-employed, work within a corporation, own multiple businesses or are officially retired, the first step towards positive change is the removal of any resistance in relation to how things currently are. Then, if you still have a desire to shift gears in your career or go in a new direction, you can remove any restraints holding you back from going for what you really want. To start the shift from 'Oh God, not another day at work' to 'Thank God, I've got another day to do my work', here are three principles that give you a happier relationship *with* your career:

Principle 1: You are not your job title

How do you know you have a job (or want a job)? In the same way that you know you have thoughts and emotions because you are aware of them, the awareness within you is also aware of the work you do. Although the name on your business card can change, the awareness within you is permanent, unchanging and the true nature of *what* you really are. Despite this reality, we often come to the conclusion that we *are what we do*. This misidentification with job titles comes partly from us not being taught about our true nature growing up and is then compounded by the societal norms that we take for granted. Have you noticed that one of the first questions we ask or are asked when meeting someone new is, 'What do you do?' With the common responses being something along the lines of 'I am an artist, architect, doctor, therapist... [*insert your job title here*]'.

Despite this casual interaction seeming relatively harmless on the surface, it is indicative of a deeper identity problem at play. Many people actually believe that they *are* what they *do* and when this happens, become prone to experiencing inner conflict. When your identity becomes intertwined with your work, the inevitable by-product is to make your career very personal and take it very seriously. Your sense of self can become reliant upon the ever-changing climate of your career and your external 'success'. Conflict is then commonplace in your work-life, as you resist anything that threatens your sense of self or negatively impacts your worth. You also become attached to getting specific outcomes and keeping your particular position. The end result: losing connection with the calm of your consciousness, fluctuating degrees of job satisfaction – depending on what's happening at work – and a significant rise in stress levels.

> *Heal your relationship with work by being your*
> *permanent self while doing your temporary tasks.*

Allow me to use my career to illustrate. On paper, I am a bestselling author. Now, if I believed this is *who* I am, I would start resisting anything that could potentially threaten or question that identity. If *Calm Cure* doesn't hit the number one spot (God forbid!), I would suffer. If I were also attached to writing my next bestseller, I might unconsciously write a watered-down message – due to a fear of it not being popular or mainstream enough – instead of freely writing the best book possible. Many people are unsatisfied with their work-life and don't perform at their very best because they've not only invested time and effort, but also their identity has also become invested in the work that they do.

Knowing *you* are not the work you do enables you to engage whatever you are doing with more flare, freedom and far less fear. You don't define yourself by your temporary job title or role, but instead draw your identity from the inner presence of peace that is permanently present inside you. Quite wonderfully, engaging your work with self-awareness makes it possible for anyone to coexist peacefully with anything that comes their way at work and perform to their highest potential.

Principle 2: You are not a slave to the system

Mortgages, utility bills and other living expenses can make us believe that we have no choice but to go to work to earn money to survive. Yet, despite the realities of modern-day spending habits and the fact that you maybe *do* have to work to keep everything afloat, it is more important than ever to adopt the attitude required for not being conflicted. Whenever you believe that you *have* to do something, you connect with a conflict-creating victim mentality that's fuelled by the perceived lack of choice. This kind of attitude has a detrimental impact upon your relationship *with* what you do. It causes you to engage work with a begrudging resistance that subtly eats away at your satisfaction, creates an array of attachments and causes an undercurrent of angst.

> *Even if you don't appear to have a*
> *choice, being at peace with what you*
> *need to do can dramatically increase*
> *your satisfaction and success.*

'But Sandy, I really don't have a choice about whether I go to work or not.' I appreciate that, but despite your external demands, nothing has the power to stop you from shifting your attitude towards life so that there is zero conflict with your current situation. It is possible to heal your relationship with it by making the move from 'I have to' to 'I choose to' – and in doing so, not feel like a victim with no choice.

CALM GAME: I CHOOSE TO...

If you can relate to this and feel that you *have* to go to work, then ask: *Ultimately, why do I choose to go to work?*

If your answer is 'to make money', then ask: *Ultimately, why do I choose to make money?* Aim to clarify higher-level motives, beyond the simple drive to make money. Examples include: To provide for my family, to put good food on the table, to have a nice home to live in or to take nice holidays, etc.

Once you've found your higher-level motive(s), ask: *Do I want to* [insert your higher-level motive]? For instance, *Do I want to provide for my family?* or *Do I want to live in a nice home?*

Upon recognizing that you *do* want the higher-level motive(s), it is a natural next step to congruently state, 'I choose to go to work.' This simple shift can radically reduce your resistance and enable you to be engaged with the 'system' without being a slave to it.

Principle 3: You are happiest when in service

Have you noticed how good it feels to know that you've made a positive difference to someone's life? Even the smallest act of service can bring a great sense of satisfaction and fulfilment. However, have you also noticed how anytime you have a problem, it usually involves a lot of 'me-type' thinking? *How is this going to affect me? How can I make sure they do what I want or give me what I need?* One of the main reasons why service feels so good is because the mind-made 'me' – consisting of all of its needs, expectations, judgements and conflicts – is put on the back burner for a while and is not your primary focus. When in service, you are instead fully focused on where you can give and how you can contribute.

There is a direct relationship between personal satisfaction and engaging life with a service-oriented attitude. If you go to work with an attitude of 'What's in it for me?' or 'What can I get?', rather than 'How can I give and be of service?' then you're far more likely to end up in conflict. You will push away what doesn't meet your expectations and be attached to getting what you think you need. However, if you engage with a 'How can I serve?' attitude, then you are much better at what you do, make a greater contribution, and end up rewarded for your positive impact.

Service to others offers the ultimate win-win scenario.

Waiting to give after you've received is a back-to-front way of working, which rarely leads to genuine satisfaction or success. On the contrary, by recognizing that you are happiest when in service to others, and looking for ways to give, give and give some more, you transform your relationship *with* the work you do *and* the results you get. When engaging my work, I focus first on how to serve others better than ever before. By doing so, I automatically gain great pleasure, and have noticed that the better I serve, the more profitable the business remains too.

Now, sometimes when suggesting this, I hear the response: *'Nice idea Sandy, but I've given too much in the past and ended up exhausted.'* However, upon deeper enquiry, in such cases, we have usually found that they have been giving in a conflicted way, which has been the real reason for their burnout. Working in the background there has been a resistance associated with what they've been doing and it has been the chronic resistance that's impacted their health and energy levels.

Giving to get back is not really giving and it doesn't create the same results or rewards. With a service-oriented attitude, you give without attachment to receiving anything in return. You know from your first-hand experience that through service you are always rewarded by how good it feels. The invitation is therefore to check in anytime you've got lots of 'me-type' thoughts going on that are causing restriction, resistance and dissatisfaction in whatever you are doing. And instead, to set the intention of being of service in any which way you can. I promise, it will improve your sense of satisfaction and transform your relationship *with* your work for the better.

TIP *Go to www.calmclan.com/career for a STRESS-FREE SUCCESS guided meditation.*

USING CALM CURE ON COMMON CAREER ISSUES

Do you recall the three ideal career standards? By applying these principles, you will fulfil the first two by making the shift from *having to* go to work to *choosing to*. While knowing that you are not your career and engaging what you do with a service-oriented attitude, you take your work-life less personally and earn great satisfaction. In the next chapter I will show you how to heal your relationship with money so that you can also earn more than you need. First, let's continue by calming common career issues.

For each of the following career issues, read the descriptions to find any that are present in your work-life. Then use the Calm Cure (*see Chapter 3, page 35*) to resolve any conflict that is causing you to create and remain connected to any of the particular problems. For example, reading the list you see that you've been in conflict with the office politics going on in your workplace. To use Calm Cure, ask: *How does the office politics make me feel?* Let's say you feel 'alone'. You would then use the rest of the technique to get peace with the office politics and encourage positive change in your working environment.

Dead-end job: Your role has limited prospects; you feel you're going nowhere and face daily doses of dullness, count the hours or hate the monotony. Even the most repetitive task can be satisfying with the right attitude. Use Calm Cure to explore how it feels to be in a 'dead-end job' and if you do want a change, clear any resistance to moving into a job that's more inspiring.

Performance pressure: You experience constant pressure to perform, work in an environment that expects every last bit of you and overwork to meet deadlines or targets – all at the detriment of your health. Stress is caused by your relationship with external expectations or demands. Use Calm Cure to reduce the pressure you feel around performing so that you can calmly complete any task that is given to you.

Office politics: Rather than being a peaceful and supportive place to be creative, connect with your colleagues and get the job done, you feel like you walk into a war zone of sly comments, undermining, bitching behind backs and covert strategizing. Conflict breeds conflict so, if you resist it, you end up engaging a similar energy to the one you would like to eradicate. Use Calm Cure to explore how the office politics makes you feel in order to be a peaceful presence and a compassionate colleague. It helps to remember that those engaged in office politics do so out of fear and insecurity and with the desire to connect and feel secure. Be the change you want to see.

Work–life imbalance: Your balance is completely off between your work and personal life. You work too hard or you play too often. Either way, it is now negatively impacting your results and you feel the need to bring your work-life back to balance. Use Calm Cure to explore how it feels to work too much or to find what you may be attempting to avoid through your almost permanent vacation.

Daily commute: You dread the daily commute and find it a painful part of your day. Remember that it's not what you are doing, but your relationship with what you are doing that determines how much you enjoy it. It is possible to experience complete contentment and utter fulfilment watching paint dry, if you are self-aware and fully present. Use Calm Cure to enjoy the journey by resolving any resistance and to ascend beyond any attachment to doing anything other than the commute.

Can't say no: Although I've encouraged you to have a service-oriented attitude, there's a big difference between being helpful and having no boundaries. If you simply can't say no, then it's time to draw a line in the sand and stop it. Use Calm Cure to explore how saying no makes you feel. Resolve the resistance to 'no' and any attachments to people-please or over-give.

Not my passion: You are in a role that involves work that you simply aren't passionate about. You try to do your best but it's an effort because you find it uninteresting or dull. You may even know that you would love to do something else, whether that be to paint, run a bed-and-breakfast in the country or work away from a desk. Use Calm Cure to clear the conflict that is causing you to keep doing things that don't make your heart sing. You will either enjoy what you do more or follow your heart along a new and interesting career path.

Retirement countdown: You are done with the whole idea of 'work' and feel ready to retire, but your diary is dictating that you stay longer. Your heart isn't in it any more; however, you believe you can't leave until someone else says it's time to receive your clichéd gold clock. When counting down to your leaving day, your options are to explore ways to leave early or get peace with working the remaining time. Use Calm Cure to clear any conflict so you aren't counting the days.

Redundancy-ready: You already know you want to move on but you stay for the sole reason that there's talk of there being a chance you might be made redundant and receive a golden handshake. Use Calm Cure to be at peace with staying or not be so attached to the prospect of a payment. Time is a precious commodity and living in a state of waiting puts your power and prospects in other people's hands.

Job insecurity: Word on the street is that there may be job losses and you really don't want to end up on the list of leavers. It is stressing you out and you're worrying whether you'll have a job next week. Acknowledge that getting stressed won't increase your chances of staying. Rather, your resistance to being 'let go of' and attachment to staying will lower your performance, and up the chances of you losing your job. Use the Calm Cure to resolve how the job insecurity makes you feel.

Job seeker: You are currently unemployed, either recently or for longer than you would like. Although the headlines or newspaper job listings may give the impression that there's nothing available, there is always work. Use Calm Cure to clear any conflict with your employment status, and you may be surprised by how quickly you start seeing opportunities and by how well you come across in interviews.

Broke self-employed: Initially you were excited about the infinite possibilities, independence and freedom that being self-employed would provide. But you are now struggling to make enough money to pay yourself for all the hard work you're putting in. In an attempt to enhance earnings it is easy to focus on the lack of moneymaking opportunities or get super-busy trying to get clients or sell more products. Use Calm Cure to gain peace with how it feels and clear any inner blocks that have been keeping you broke.

Out of reach: You feel what you want isn't possible, to the extent that there's no point even trying. Although your mind may come up with some convincing evidence and make you feel justified to believe as you do, using Calm Cure to get peace with the inner experience can make your goals feel closer and more achievable.

Burned before: You've been let down in the past, some things you've tried haven't worked out or someone has double-crossed you or taken advantage, for example. This makes you feel dubious and reluctant to 'get back in the ring' and try again. Use Calm Cure to get peace with past let-downs or failures, and fearlessly *go for it!*

Pecking order: There's a hierarchy within your workplace and you are in conflict with not being as high up as you would like. Or perhaps you feel taken advantage of, treated badly or ignored by those higher up. Whatever your reason for resisting the organizational structure, use Calm Cure to get peace with it and resolve all that's preventing you from being promoted into a higher pay grade.

Transition Period

Has it become evident that you want to change jobs or start a new business or career? Unless you have a big pile of cash in the bank or under your bed, I don't recommend going in to work tomorrow with your resignation letter. Whether we like it or not, we live in a world that requires us to have money for food, shelter and almost everything else. If you do want to make a career change, then it will involve a transition period. It is helpful to use Calm Cure to be at peace with the time it may take to head in a new direction.

At the other end of the spectrum are those who want to make a change but never get around to doing anything about it. I've met many people who say they want change, but don't make it happen. Rome wasn't built in a day, but brick by brick. Commit to doing something every day, irrespective of how small, to make the move towards the work-life you want. It's amazing how quickly things change and how the people, events and things you need start showing up, if you meet the world halfway.

BORN TO BE

When no longer governed by the constraints of conditioning, we naturally gravitate towards certain gifts, talents, abilities, purposes and passions. Unfortunately, few fulfil their purpose because they get conditioned to be someone and do something else. Despite their natural gift for playing the violin, they are raised in a family of doctors and end up going into a similar field as their father. Or they are born into a community that cringes when anyone steps outside the social norms and so compromise their heart to stay with the herd.

Not living your purpose is a very corrosive form of conflict.

It's hard to know what your purpose is as long as you rely on your head to tell you. Your purpose may be something you've never done or even heard of before. But your mind can only make suggestions based upon the past and what it's learned. Getting caught up in the conditioning of the mind has proved, time after time, to be a very limited way to live for many. However, engaging life from self-awareness, you become able to see the signs that life is giving you and are willing to let life take you in directions you could never have imagined.

By being self-aware and present it becomes glaringly obvious for those with eyes to see, that every moment we are being guided towards our purpose. With self-awareness, you rise above the conflicting chatter of the mind to access the inner calm and clarity that make it possible to hear the voice of your intuitive wisdom. It becomes super-clear what's right for you and what is just a distraction. Perhaps most beautifully, you get to see that the present moment is always presenting your perfect purpose and all you need to do for the most wonderful work-life is to walk towards it and play your part fully.

 TIP *For more support and free resources to apply the principles of Calm Cure to your CAREER, visit my Calm Clan: www.calmclan.com/career*

Chapter 8

MONEY

Frustrated to Free

Money: the root of all kinds of evil or a route to enlightenment and personal freedom? With the right attitude and relationship *with* money, I believe it's the latter. If we define money in terms of physical currencies such as bank notes, coins and cash deposited in bank accounts, there's currently around $80 trillion kicking about. Whereas if we include other forms of nonphysical money – including digital currency Bitcoin and funds invested in financial products like derivatives – then the total runs into the quadrillions (that's 15 zeros!).[6] This means that money is both a physical and a nonphysical entity. The reason I raise this is that the nature of money is very relevant to how we relate to it. We all have an objective (physical/outer) and a subjective (nonphysical/inner) experience of money. Said slightly differently, we have the objective reality of how much money we physically possess and a subjective inner experience of how it feels to have that amount of money.

To comprehend the importance of this distinction, consider *why* you want money. Common answers include: to buy things, like property, cars, food, holidays etc. and so I can feel safe, secure, happy and free. These responses clearly show that there are objective financial desires like property and holidays, and subjective fiscal aspirations like security and freedom. Unfortunately, growing up it is common to accumulate a massive amount of conditioning that messes with our inner experience of, and relationship with, money.

Collectively, we have come to rely upon money to define our sense of self and to feel safe, secure, valuable and free. This strategy will never work because if we seek these subjective experiences from outside means, then they will forever be dependent on fluctuating financial conditions. This dependency on money again creates conflict, so it therefore pays dividends to invest in improving our subjective inner relationship with money – if we want our financial experience to improve. In short, millions of people have made money way too important and a rebalancing of power is needed to return to a more sane and serene coexistence with it.

> *'Money is our madness, our vast collective madness.'*
> D. H. LAWRENCE

FINANCIALLY FREE

Those frustrated by the amount of money they have and who consistently find it hard to make more, tend to have a conflicted inner experience of, and relationship with, money. The same goes for people with money who are worried about losing it. Our inner world is the platform on which we build our outer world. With the right inner foundation, you can move from frustration or fear to feeling financially free. Here are three principles that can provide an abundant attitude and a liberated relationship *with* money.

Principle 1: You can feel secure without financial security

All three 'money principles' have the power of intention at the heart of them. Your intention is the subtler reasoning behind *why* you want what you think you want. Intent is so important because it has a subjective emotional element, which has a big impact upon what we create in the external world. Meaning, even if you are doing your best to engage the right strategies to make or maintain money, if your undercover intentions are not aligned with what you want, you'll end up getting your intent rather than your intended outcome. Applying the power of intention to your financial life involves ensuring that your monetary aspirations are therefore aligned with your intent for why you want it. When fully aligned, subjectively you can be a master manifestor in your objective world.

The search for financial security

One of the most widely held reasons for wanting money is to have 'financial security'. Can you relate to wanting to feel secure? Being safe and secure is a primary concern for most people. However, attempting to acquire an inner sense of security from externally obtained money is a risky and ineffective strategy, which creates inner conflict. If you need money in order to be secure then you will resist not having as much as you think you need and be attached to the magical amount that you believe will deliver the security you're searching for.

At the heart of this kind of conflict is fear and insecurity and the presence of experiences that you may be in conflict with, such as being incapable, uncertain, or having no control etc. Until you heal the conflict experience, you will have an incongruent intent that is contrary to what you want, i.e. there will be an intention *not* to be uncertain, which is what you will unconsciously move towards, for example. If you can relate to this need for externally sought secureness, then use Calm Cure to resolve it (*see Chapter 3, page 35*). The aim is to be able to remain secure without any fixed financial requirements propping up your sense of security. Alongside the Calm Cure, you can feel more unconditionally secure by engaging life from self-awareness – using the GAAWO technique (*see Chapter 2, page 21*). Your awareness is the ultimate safe and secure space to live from and is present within you, irrespective of your bank balance.

Principle 2: You can feel worthy without financial wealth

Self-esteem, worthiness and personal value are also often linked with financial wealth. Before discovering this, my self-esteem would rise and fall depending on the digits appearing on my bank statements. If it were a more abundant month, I would walk around with my head held high and a significant sense of self-worth. However, if there was a dip in the digits and money reserves were running below my ideal amount then I would feel somewhat 'less than', inferior to those with bigger bank accounts, and question my standing in society.

I've observed that countless others have also linked their self-worth with how much money they happen to have. With money they feel more of a person of value, or if they have less than the next person, they feel a less valuable member of society. This sentiment is supported by many societal norms, as we live in a world that tends to make rich people more important than those less well off. Despite this, we are all born equal and remain that way, irrespective of our financial standing.

> *'Never confuse the size of your pay packet*
> *with the size of your talent.'*
> MARLON BRANDO

Similar to security, if because of your conditioning you have been basing your self-worth upon external means, then use Calm Cure to clear any conflict experiences that may be leading to you feeling anything other than wholly worthy and valuable. *How does not having as much money as other people make you feel?* The goal is to know deeply that you are a person of value, full stop, not because you are rich, live in a big house, drive a fancy car or shop in high-end stores. Gaining this rock-solid self-worth that is free from your current financial status is vital if you want to make more money. If you believe you are unworthy of having more, then you will continue with the levels of financial prosperity that reflect what you think you deserve. But by clearing this conditioning, and again engaging your invaluable self-awareness, you can increase your self-worth while also improving your net worth.

Principle 3: You can feel free without financial freedom

Calm Cure's strategy for financial freedom doesn't focus on having 'loads-a-money', but having a willingness to experience the full spectrum of financial possibilities, from rich to poor and everything in between. I appreciate that this might be a big thing to explore. But remember, you move towards and remain connected to what you are focused upon and in conflict with. If you're at the lower income end, then by applying this new strategy you can more easily move up the spectrum. For the record, if you consider yourself to be rather rich, then fear not, this strategy won't cause you to lose money either. It just means that if your financial situation does happen to change, then you won't suffer. It's a win-win. You see, if a person does have a more traditional idea of financial freedom, but is scared of losing their money, then they aren't really free.

During my journey towards being financially free, it didn't matter how much money I had because I noticed I never enjoyed it or felt free. I spent my days swinging from frustration to fear. Frustrated because I didn't have enough yet and then when I achieved my financial goals, I immediately swung into feeling scared about losing what I'd worked so hard to get. Applying this new strategy for financial freedom is the best strategy for avoiding this kind of fear-based relationship with money.

Enjoying financial freedom involves using Calm Cure to clear any conflict towards experiencing the complete spectrum of financial possibilities. To do this, start by exploring how it would make you feel to be on the 'poor' end and use the rest of the technique to get peace with that possibility. Then do the same for the 'rich' end. Even if you've never experienced it before, it is of real value to clear any conflict that you may have towards being abundant. (When I did this I discovered fears about being 'caught out by the tax man' and feelings of guilt at having more than my friends or family.) Consider how it would make you feel to have vast amounts of money. Give it a go and let yourself be liberated from what might be standing between you and inner and outer financial freedom.

> *'Wealth is the ability to fully experience life.'*
> HENRY DAVID THOREAU

CALM GAME: MONEY MEDITATION

In *Body Calm*, I introduced a meditation technique that can be used to help the body to rest, improve the communication between the mind and body, and also heal unhealthy beliefs. The meditation technique includes engaging GAAWO (*see Chapter 2, page 21*) and thinking a series of 10 Calm thoughts. To cultivate an abundant attitude, there are actually three of the Calm thoughts that are perfect for healing your beliefs:

- *I am secure* (focus on the soles of the feet)

- *I am worthy* (focus on the top of the head)

- *I am free* (focus in your forehead centre)

You will see from the above list that each of the Calm thoughts has three words that you think – *I am secure*, for example – and also a focus point to direct your attention while thinking it, such as the soles of the feet. By thinking the words with your focus in the recommended location, the Calm thoughts end up being a very powerful tool for cultivating new attitudes. To get the best results, it is recommended you use them with your eyes open, for what I call 'Calm Moments' and also with your eyes closed, during

Calm Sittings (see below). Similar to money, the more you invest in doing both open- and closed-eye Calm, the bigger the returns.

To have a Calm Moment, simple engage GAAWO for a few seconds before thinking one of the Calm thoughts. Then having done so simply let go of the words and focus point by re-engaging GAAWO. Then continue with your day until the next time you remember to have a Calm Moment. For Calm Moments, choose a daily or weekly 'default' Calm thought to use. Here are the instructions for closed-eye Calm Sittings:

Calm Sitting

Sit comfortably and close your eyes.

Step 1: Engage GAAWO (Gently Alert Attention Wide Open).

Step 2: Think a Calm thought (including the focus point).

Step 3: Engage GAAWO (Gently Alert Attention Wide Open).

Repeat the cycle when you notice you've been off thinking.

Let me guide you through a 'Money Meditation' Calm Sitting:

- Begin by sitting comfortably, close your eyes, and engage GAAWO by being gently alert with your attention wide open. Hang out for a few moments before the next step.

- Think *I am secure*, with your attention on the soles of your feet... Let go of the words and focus point by re-engaging GAAWO. Rest consciously aware until you notice you've been off thinking about other things.

- Then engage GAAWO for a short while before thinking, *I am worthy*, with your attention on the top of your head... Let go of the words and the focus point by re-engaging GAAWO.

Rest consciously aware until you notice you've been off thinking about other things.

- Then engage GAAWO for a short while before thinking, *I am free*, with your attention in your forehead centre... Let go of the words and the focus point by re-engaging GAAWO. Rest consciously aware until you notice you've been off thinking about other things.

- If you are ready to end your Calm Sitting, slowly open your eyes. If you would like to continue for longer (the recommended Calm Sitting duration is 10–20 minutes), repeat the cycle of the three Calm thoughts following the above steps.

 Tip *Go to www.calmclan.com/money to be guided through this MONEY meditation.*

USING CALM CURE ON COMMON MONEY ISSUES

Our conditioning surrounding money can crop up in several ways, such as regretting 'bad' financial decisions, the compulsion to overspend or how you feel about being in debt. I recommend reading through the following list of common money issues. For the one(s) you relate to, use the Calm Cure to be financially free.

Family finances: Were you raised in a family that had 'issues' over money? Common comments made may have included 'money doesn't grow on trees' or 'I'm not made of money'. Or perhaps you were fed beliefs like, 'there's no such thing as a free lunch' or 'money isn't easy to make'. Were your parents very secretive about money, clingy with their cash or did you sense anguish every time a bill dropped on the doormat? Use Calm Cure to heal any lingering beliefs or feelings you may have picked up from family around money.

Bad decisions: Have you made bad decisions that have caused you to lose money or miss out on making more? Are you still berating yourself that you should have known better? Do you feel shame, regret or guilt for losing money that you'd planned to use for retirement or leave as inheritances for those you cherish most? Or perhaps you invested in a business that didn't work out and you regret the decision to this day. Use Calm Cure to get peace with any past financial decisions.

Greedy bankers: Many economists consider the global financial crisis of 2007–09 to be the worst monetary disaster since the Great Depression of the 1930s. Thousands of people lost a lot of money, some even their homes, and to this day there is much animosity and anger towards the 'bankers'. Use Calm Cure to get peace with how the 'crisis' and any other fallout from it made you feel.

Relentless recessions: Turn on your television or read the newspaper and you'll find a steady stream of reports including fears over recessions, new austerity cuts, redundancies and labour cutbacks, etc. This bad news can all feed a lack mentality along with a need to protect, hoard and survive instead of thrive. Use the Calm Cure on how it feels to be in a recession.

Credit history: If you have a bad credit score, then it can not only impact your ability to get finance, but can also affect your sense of self-worth and confidence. Explore how having a lower score than society states is 'good' makes you feel and use Calm Cure to clear any conflict with your current rating.

Decades of debt: The interesting thing about humanity's collective relationship with money is that we often spend more than we have. The global debt sits at just under $200 trillion, which, based upon 'real' money, is much more than what physically exists. When in debt it can be hard to see how you're ever going to be free, especially if you find it hard even to pay the interest. Many people with mortgages can also end up postponing their peace and happiness until they make their final payment. Debt can create conflict experiences that don't actually help us to get out of the red. Use Calm Cure to heal how it feels to be in debt.

Bankruptcy anonymous: Being made bankrupt can be a big relief when it finally happens because at least the people chasing you for money can no longer send you nasty letters. However, for some it can be seen as a big failure to be ashamed of. No, you don't have a credit card for the time being, but do you really want one? It's an opportunity to heal your relationship with money and feel free whatever your spending power. Use Calm Cure to get peace with going bankrupt and to help it not to happen again.

Nice or necessary: One of the main reasons so many people always need more money or end up in debt is because they buy much more stuff than they actually need. One quick way to check in with yourself before spending again is to ask: *Is what I'm about to buy nice or necessary?* Obviously you are free to buy 'nice' things, but it can help you be more mindful as you do. Most of the stuff we are buying is not for the thing itself, but how we believe the thing might make us feel – or not feel. Explore what feelings you are trying to buy (or avoid) and use the Calm Cure on the compulsion to spend, spend, spend.

Meet Martin, who was a serial spender

Martin loved to spend money. It didn't matter how much he earned, there was never any left at the end of the month. When asked, 'How does the thought of not buying stuff make you feel?' He responded, 'Pointless, purposeless and alone.' He recalled these feelings showing up when he was a teenager and shared how he always felt like the outsider at school, was never invited to parties and was often at home at the weekend feeling very lonely because he had nothing to do. Using step 2 of Calm Cure, he rated 3/10 for his willingness to have things to do sometimes and have nothing to do sometimes.

We used Calm Past to help him find the knowings: 'I am good company, I have friends that invite me to do stuff these days and I actually choose to go shopping instead of hanging out.' When testing the memory, he still felt some resistance to having nothing to do so we used Calm Future. He then realized that the 'future me' had discovered the value in spending time with people he loved, instead of spending money. Having installed this knowing he was then willing to have things to do sometimes, and sometimes not, and went on to say, 'The thought of it doesn't make me feel lonely any more.'

Catching up with Martin a few months later, he shared that he didn't feel the compulsion to spend, was enjoying his time alone and around others more, and had started to accumulate savings.

Retirement fund: You worry about if you will have stored enough savings and/or investments for your retirement. It's the focus of your attention, brings up fear and may even keep you working more than is healthy. Many of the fears we have over a retirement fund are fed to us by the news and advertisers. It is obviously wise to plan ahead, but not so much that you aren't enjoying today. Use Calm Cure to clear the fear associated with running out before you check out.

The 1 per cent club: Global financial inequality is growing with half of the world's wealth in the hands of only one per cent of the population. Just over 70 per cent of the global adult population (3.4 billion people) has wealth of less than US$10,000.[7] How does that make you feel? Use Calm Cure to resolve feelings of unfairness, anger, etc., about the unequal distribution of global wealth.

ENOUGH IS ENOUGH

Several years ago, I was scheduled to meet three different members of the same family at my London clinic. Waiting for them to arrive I remember enjoying a few moments of calm while gazing out of my window, which looked out over the car park and then beyond into Richmond Park. I will never forget what happened next. One by one, three brand new Bentleys entered the car park and majestically lined up side by side. After what appeared to be a synchronized opening of car doors, out stepped the family members I was about to meet.

Over the next couple of hours I met them privately and began each consultation with my usual exploratory question: 'What do you want more than anything else?' To which they answered, 'Peace, contentment and happiness.' But the fascinating thing, and the reason for sharing this, was that when I then asked, 'How are you getting on enjoying an ongoing experience of what you ultimately want?' They all had a similar response of, 'Not very well.' It turned out, despite their riches, they lacked an abundant life experience.

> *'There are people who have money*
> *and people who are rich.'*
> COCO CHANEL

It isn't revolutionary news to hear that money doesn't make us happy; it's almost a cliché these days. Nonetheless, have you taken on board this reality? Or are you still striving to make more money so that you can eventually feel fulfilled? Money is a carrot – making us run for our lives towards a future filled with all the things we think we need to be happy.

You need *no* thing to be happy. Cut the strings of your attachment to needing more by recognizing that there is a difference between being abundant and having lots of money. Abundance is an inner state of being that can be accessed immediately with the right attitude and by engaging this moment with self-awareness. By being present and willing to experience the full spectrum of financial possibilities, you can discover that you have more than you need and enough is enough.

 TIP *For more support and free resources to apply the principles of Calm Cure to MONEY, visit my Calm Clan: www.calmclan.com/money*

Chapter 9

TIME

Bounded to Beyond

We are generally living longer. Yet despite the extra years on planet Earth, an increasing proportion of the population are stressed by their schedules and believe they don't have enough time. Year on year since 2001, in the Gallup lifestyle study, around 50 per cent of Americans report they don't have enough time.[8] How would you respond to the survey? Would you say you have ample time or do you feel squeezed by your schedule? Why do so many of us end up chasing our tails with an apparent lack of time? How do we end up trapped by time – dwelling on the past, not being able to fit everything in or fretting about the future? If you are running from one thing to the next or find that you regularly feel sad, stressed or anxious, then it is time to heal your relationship *with* time.

> *Healing your relationship with time starts*
> *by being here and now in the timeless*
> *reality of the present moment.*

In *Mind Calm* I introduced the idea of the 'Time Trap' when talking about why we spend so much time thinking about the past and future. The Time Trap is subtle and stems from the belief that the past or future are *relevant* to experiencing what we ultimately want in life – whether that is peace, love, happiness or achieving certain goals. Quite simply, if we believe what happened in the past or might happen in the future is relevant to our current sense of self, wellness and success, we will feel compelled to think forever about the past and future. However, when we stop pausing the present to go into the past or fixating on the future, we can instantly be free from many time-based problems.

ALL THE TIME IN THE WORLD

One of the main reasons why so many people don't feel they have enough time is because they aren't present. They waste a huge amount of time overthinking about the past and future, which then causes them to miss the only moment that matters – when they can actually get anything done. Also, when missing the moment and caught up in the mind, they end up feeling their thinking. If their thoughts happen to be about upsetting past events or scary future possibilities, then that is how they inevitably end up feeling.

So if you feel bound by tight deadlines, don't feel you can get enough done, experience anxiety or concern about what might happen and know you often miss the moment, here are three principles for healing your relationship with time.

Principle 1: The past is only a medley of memories

Without inventing a time machine, you cannot change what's happened in the past. By this point, you will have a multitude of memories, ranging from the radiant to the ridiculous and the sad to the serene. Some you will be delighted to have experienced. Others you may wish had never happened and could vanish from your mind forever. Despite your perspective on what's happened during the years leading up to now, reducing your attraction to dwelling on the past can save time.

Mind-made memories

Healing your relationship with time requires recognizing that the past isn't happening in the reality of now, but only ever in your mind. Memories are a type of thought and the past is simply a collection of thought-based memories. When you view memories as thoughts, it stops the past from being so real, relevant or distressing. You discover that the past becomes a problem when you leave the present moment to feel your thoughts about a previous time that isn't happening any more.

With this understanding, you will see the big benefits of being here now and no longer entertaining thoughts about the past. Now, I appreciate some memories can feel very real and give the impression that present-day peace isn't possible *because* of what happened. But the truth is your memories are no more real than anything else you can conjure up using your imagination. If you are willing to let go of your past-based thoughts to reside in the current reality, they stop possessing power to impact you negatively today. You can be free from the past, the moment you engage present-moment awareness.

> *You stop being a victim to your past when you know it only negatively impacts you when you think about it now.*

For any past memories that you feel compelled to think about, and bring up negative emotions when you do, then use the Calm Cure (*see Chapter 3, page 35*) to clear any conflict towards what happened. Unresolved memories are simply previous event(s) that you are *still* in conflict with. If any memory generates anger, sadness, hurt, fear, guilt, grief, shame, remorse or any discomfort when thinking about it, then you are holding on to some kind of conflict in relation to it. You are resisting what happened because you remain attached to something else happening instead: *My dad should have stayed. My mum should have been more loving. I shouldn't have failed at that business.* When releasing yourself from the prison of the past, the first step is always to recognize that memories are just thoughts that you are giving far too much attention. Then with self-awareness and the Calm Cure technique, bring conscious calm to the memories that you've been unconsciously in conflict with. Doing so will cause you to dwell on the past far less and free up your focus for the present moment.

Principle 2: The future is only a fantasy

Similarly to the past, without investing in a time machine you cannot transport yourself to the future to find out what's going to happen. We think we know what's going to happen, but we really don't. Despite this, billions of people are wasting hundreds of hours every year thinking about the future. Completely caught up in fictitious fantasies about what *might* happen, they are missing the only moment during which they can actually take any action and create the life they want. Just imagine if you could stop thinking so much about future scenarios and focus all of your attention on now. How much more effective and productive would you be, if you gave 100 per cent of yourself to being your potential now?

I was once invited to memorize and then recite word for word a document consisting of several thousands words, as part of a course I attended. It wasn't until I sat down to memorize it that I saw how scattered my attention was, as I habitually drifted off into future-based thoughts. I would be looking at the words on the page, while also thinking ahead, e.g. 'This is impossible.' 'It's too much to remember.' 'I will never be able to do this.' To my surprise, when I gave all of my attention to the word I was memorizing, I recited it all perfectly. The exercise showed me how we can tap into a potential way beyond what we believe is possible, when we are fully present.

The future only exists in your imagination and is just another type of thought. I agree it can feel real or intimidating when thinking about it, but it is no more real than the past. So why do we waste so much time thinking about it? Usually because we fear what might happen – and are resistant to the full spectrum of life possibilities or attached to specific outcomes. We plan, strategize and think at length about countless conceivable scenarios to avoid certain things happening and ensure we get what we think we need. Remember, this kind of living has its foundations in conflict and also distracts us from the only moment that exists, and that has the power to determine the results we get.

> *Anxiety can become a thing of the past when*
> *you stop fantasizing about the future.*

Knowing that the future is only a collection of thoughts that happen in your mind can be a complete game-changer for anyone suffering from chronic fear or anxiety. You can see that any concern you have about future events is not due to what might happen, but by thinking *about* what might happen. Read that again. When you know your fear or anxiety are not because of the 'bad' things that might happen, but by feeling your thinking, you stop being a victim to future possibilities. You can be free from the future by engaging present-moment awareness and using the Calm Cure to explore any possible experiences you are in conflict with. As you reduce your resistance and attachment towards the future, you won't feel the need to think about it so much. You will be able to give your fullest attention to now and in doing so, be far more effective and fearless.

Principle 3: The present is the only moment that exists

Time is always limited. With 60 minutes per hour and 24 hours in any given day, as long as you live within the parameters of time, you will remain bounded by the constant countdown of the nearest ticking clock. Time is also a mind-made construct that, in reality, doesn't actually exist. Yes there is day and night and time can be useful for meeting a friend or catching a movie, yet there is ultimately no such thing as 9 a.m., for example. Time can feel like it is slipping away, running out, and can cause stress when we forget this truth. But when you let go of the concept of time to return all of your attention to *now*, you immediately go beyond its linear borders and boundaries to experience the timeless reality of the present moment. I choose to refer to it as 'real-ity', as a reminder that *this* moment is the only 'time' that is *real*. By letting go of the limits of time, you spend more time in reality and discover in your own experience that *this* moment is the only one that exists.

Do you want to experience real life or spend the majority of your days in a melody of memories or fictitious fantasies?

The choice to live a real life, instead of wasting time thinking about stuff that isn't even happening, can be yours with self-awareness. Awareness is only aware of what is happening now. Engaging GAAWO and aligning with your inner awareness, you become present. Better still, you will also be amazed how much you can get done and by how little stress you feel. You can discover that stress is not due to a lack of time or a long things-to-do-list, but by leaving the moment to think about everything that *needs* to be done. By being here now and giving all of your attention to the task in hand, you can calmly get on with whatever needs doing before moving on to the next thing and then the next. It's how I calmly coexist with my busy schedule and I can confirm that it works!

Today, as I write Calm Cure, the deadline for the manuscript is imminent. If I were to leave the moment to go into my mind and think about how little time I have then I would not only feel under pressure, but while thinking about the deadline I wouldn't actually be getting any good writing done! However, by focusing on each and every word, the words turn into sentences, then into paragraphs and pages. There is no benefit whatsoever in thinking about the chapters that still need to be written. The best strategy is to remain calm, write *this* word and, like magic, the task will be completed and to a higher standard than if I were super-stressed. Play with engaging in everything you do with present-moment awareness. See how much more you accomplish by being here now and not being distracted or disheartened by moving into the past or future via your mind's imagination.

 **TIP** *Go to www.calmclan.com/time for a BEING HERE NOW guided meditation.*

USING CALM CURE ON COMMON TIME ISSUES

If you do still encounter any stress in relation to time, use Calm Cure to explore how the perceived lack of time makes you feel. You may have multiple plates spinning with limited time to do it all, but there will also be a conflict experience that, when calmed, can transform your relationship with time, forever! I recommend using the Calm Cure on these common time issues:

Conflicting calendar: One of the most common causes of feeling overwhelmed and constrained by time is having multiple conflicting things to do. You are doing one thing, but you also think you should be doing something else.[9] The reality is you can only ever do one thing right now. So choose what that is and get on with it. Use Calm Cure to explore how it makes you feel to be pulled in multiple directions.

Let-downs: We don't always get what we think we want. We now know life is happening on a spectrum of possibilities. However, some past disappointments can pull us down further than others, if we don't resolve the conflict connected to them. Don't give away your power by making your let-downs *about* the person/people who let you down. Use Calm Cure to reduce the resistance to what happened and go beyond whatever you were attached to, but didn't get.

Problem parents: Having done therapy with hundreds of people, it's rare for the topic of 'parents' not to be raised at some point. I appreciate it may be an understatement to say that your parents may not have been all that you hoped for. But the precious life they gave you can be so much better if you do the inner work to coexist calmly *with* the way they raised you and/or how they are today. Explore: *How do your parents make you feel?* Clarify the conflict experience and use Calm Cure to get peace with it.

Destructive dwelling: Dwelling occurs when you stop having a natural human reaction to the stuff that happens, getting lost in your mind-made story and emotions about the past, over a prolonged period of time. If you still feel upset days, weeks or months later, and there is mental, emotional or physical suffering going on, then you are dwelling. Use Calm Cure to explore how what happened made you feel, and move on. Remember, it is only happening in your mind – the moment has already moved on!

Scary movies: We've discovered that 'negative' past events or scary future scenarios are figments of the imagination. Despite this, they can feel very real, especially if your mind feels justified to resist it and be attached to certain outcomes. For anything playing on your mind, explore how it makes you feel, find the conflict experience and use Calm Cure to be free from the movies of the mind.

The illusion of later: 'I will do it later, tomorrow, soon, one day...' Procrastination is a problem for a multitude of well-intentioned people. Whenever you are procrastinating you are buying into the belief that *later* exists. It doesn't. Now is the only moment you can do anything. If you are constantly planning to do things later and never actually get around to doing any of them, then you are essentially planning to do things at a time that will never happen in reality. How does the thought of taking action now make you feel? Clear the conflict to massively increase your present-moment-performance, and stop waiting for a time that will never come.

THE GIFT THAT KEEPS GIVING

Living in the present moment is the greatest gift you can give yourself. It is, without exaggeration, the gift that keeps giving. Right now, the forces of creation are combining to give birth to a brand new moment bursting with purpose and potential. If you have ever been confused as to what your purpose is, then you need look no further than *this* moment. Your purpose is being presented to you, right now. Reading this book is your present purpose. Beyond that, engage every moment assuming that all that is presented to you *is* exactly what you should be doing.

This attitude can transform your relationship with time. Instead of forcing your will on life and trying to get what you think will make you happy, you let life reveal your perfect purpose. As long as you don't resist what happens, you will feel fulfilled and do what you came here to do.

Being present also enables you to access your potential. Instead of getting caught up in limiting thinking, you become free to be and do whatever life is inviting you to become and achieve. I was diagnosed with dyslexia and was petrified of public speaking. Since living life with self-awareness, I've written several bestselling books and enjoy a wonderful career speaking to audiences of all sizes. To stop being bound by time, be here now and clear any conflict causing you to overthink about the past and future. It is the quickest way to be effective and enjoy every minute of your existence.

 TIP *For more support and free resources to apply the principles of Calm Cure to TIME, visit my Calm Clan: www.calmclan.com/time*

Chapter 10

WORLD

Pissed Off to Proactive

According to the 2016 Global Peace Index (GPI), which ranks 163 independent states and territories by their present levels of peacefulness, only 10 countries in the world are currently not at war. Militarism and violence are costing 13.3 per cent of the world Gross Domestic Product (GDP) – which is the equivalent of US$1,876/year for every person on the planet – and between 2007 and 2015 the numbers displaced by war doubled to around 60 million refugees.[10] On the domestic front, the UK saw a 27 per cent increase in violent crimes and a 36 per cent jump in sexual offences during 2015–16.[11] Many members of society are suffering from the austerity cuts to local services and, for a second time, the country has a Prime Minister whom the population didn't vote for at a general election. Based upon the statistics, the problems within politics, and even the warnings about global warming, the world's state of affairs look pretty bleak.

What can be done to heal the world? How can we stop killing each other and live in peace? How can we be less affected by the spectrum of economic, political, environmental and societal events? How can we move from being pissed off, upset or scared to being a proactive and peaceful presence in the world? It is easy to look out at the world and feel powerless with regard to our ability to make any worthwhile impact. It can all seem way too big a task to undertake, or appear outside our control and in the hands of others. However, if we allow ourselves to remain paralysed by our perceived powerlessness, then the world will end up being governed and shaped by the minority of people we give our power to. If these people aren't consciously aware enough to bring about positive changes based in love, freedom and the collective good, then the next generation will be left to deal with the ramifications of our reluctance to step up, wake up and bring about a better world.

The foundation of world peace is personal peace.

BE WHAT YOU WANT TO SEE

With the right attitude and relationship *with* life, it is possible for the average person to find peace. I know this is true because of my own experience: from having chronic anxiety to now being consistently calm and from witnessing the transformations in the people I've helped be more peaceful too. If it is possible for the individual, then the potential exists for peace to be reached in families, communities and countries too. Before using Calm Cure (*see Chapter 3, page 35*) to heal your relationship with anything that's bothering you about the world, here are three principles that can provide an empowered attitude, which is the precursor for moving from being pissed off to proactive.

Principle 1: World conflict reflects personal conflict

'I am proud to be one of the millions of human beings on planet Earth with the intention to live in peace and have a positive impact on the lives of others.' After posting this quote on Facebook, it quickly became my most shared meme of 2016. If you too want peace, then you are not alone. The comforting reality is that despite the stats on war suggesting the contrary, we are the majority. However, this begs the big question: If there are more people on the planet wanting calm instead of conflict, why is there not global peace? When attempting to answer this, it would be easy to blame the politicians, religions, or bullet- and bomb-makers. Yet, although they clearly contribute to making the problems possible, they aren't the ultimate cause.

> *The world reflects the collective conflict*
> *happening within the heart of humanity.*

One truth shared by many spiritual teachers is that the 'outer reflects the inner' and 'as above, so below'. The world is a reflection of the individuals who populate it. As long as there is conflict going on at an individual level, conflict will continue in the external world too. Greed, unworthiness or lack within the individual will be reflected as debt and poverty in the world. The absence of unconditional love within the individual will be mirrored back by hate in the headlines. If there is division and a sense of separateness within the individual, then countries will need borders and police to patrol them. As long as humanity places God in the sky and ignores the divinity that exists within, there will be wars fought over whose God is most righteous. This long-standing spiritual truth can be linked to many problems we see on the planet. If we want to be part of the solution, it is vital that we all play our part by calming inner conflict so that a more loving and peaceful world can be reflected back.

Let me be clear. It is not your fault. None of this has anything to do with blame, guilt or carrying the weight of the world on your shoulders. It's about reclaiming your power to make a difference and, as Mahatma Gandhi once encouraged, 'Be the change you want to see in the world.' But where do you start?

Have you noticed how different people have differing concerns about the world? You may be concerned by climate change, whereas animal cruelty distresses your friend, while your neighbour is angered by the cuts at the local hospital. I don't believe this is by chance or just down to our conditioning. We are not meant to 'heal' the world on our own. We are in it together and make our contributions depending on what is 'up for us' the most. Notice what jumps out from the tapestry of world tasks requiring some love and attention and assume it is up for *you* because there may be some inner work you can do to help. It is an opportunity to 'be the change you want to see' and serve humanity. View it as a sacred invitation to do your bit, make a contribution and impact the greater good.

Principle 2: The world exists to elevate you

For you to be reading this book (and make it to Chapter 10), there's a very high chance that you've come to the conclusion at some point that you really want to experience more calm, clarity, confidence, love, happiness, freedom, or some other positive mental, emotional or physical state or circumstance. A line in the sand has been drawn and you have committed to making positive changes to yourself, your life and in the world. The good news is that life is on your side and is currently giving you what you need to achieve your goal. I appreciate it doesn't always look or feel like this is the case. It may seem like the complete opposite. Nonetheless, it is empowering to be open to the possibility that the entire cosmos is conspiring to help you to be more loving, peaceful, abundant, healthy, etc. Continuing without this attitude, you can accidentally remain a victim of circumstance and end up in a relentless battle with life and the wider world.

The world constantly reflects your resistances and attachments. Having decided that you want something different, it starts highlighting any unconscious conflicts standing in the way of you experiencing what you want. Explaining this, a meditation teacher friend once said, 'If I had a big chunk of spinach in my teeth, then I would want someone to tell me.' In a similar way, you want life to highlight your hidden conflicts so that you can see them, heal them and let them go. In the quest to love more unconditionally, life will present people that help you to see your conditioned judgements, criticisms and criteria for love. If you want to be more abundant, then you will find yourself in situations that help you to recognize the habits preventing you from being prosperous. Or if you wish to heal a condition, you will be given events and experiences that highlight any conflicts causing your physical problem.

Through this recognition that life doesn't have a vendetta against you and by assuming that the world is reflecting your resistances and attachments, you gain a more harmonious relationship *with* what happens, which – as you've previously learned – enables the external world to change. A powerful way to do this is to make a minor change to a common question that often crops up when a person is harbouring a victim-mentality. Instead of asking: *Why is this happening* to *me?*, ask: *Why is this happening* for *me?* Although it's not a drastic change of wording, playing with this myself (after it was suggested by my Spiritual Teacher), I've found the difference is dramatic.

Exploring why something is happening *for* you allows you to see any metaphorical spinach in your teeth, that you've been oblivious to. You don't even need to find an immediate answer to the question for it to be of benefit. Simply asking: *Why is this happening for me?* has a way of improving your relationship with whatever is showing up.

When I first got into this field of work, I was faced with a steady stream of people challenging how young I was. My age continued to prevent me from making a bigger impact until I saw that it was *me* who believed my age was a disadvantage. When I stopped being in conflict with my youthfulness, nobody questioned it again. Was it a coincidence or magic? Or was it because the spiritual teachers weren't lying when they said the outer reflects the inner? If the world is in fact mirroring what's going on inside you, what conflict(s) are you being invited to be free from and wake up tomorrow without?

Principle 3: The world is the context of your awakening

The stats shared in the beginning of this chapter, about war, crime rates etc., make for pretty bleak reading. But allow me to put the world affairs into a bigger context, which I've found can improve our relationship *with* what's going on. I remember having a conversation with my original teacher of meditation – Narain Ishaya – about all the terrible things I saw occurring within the world. Sharing my concerns, sadness, and fear for the future of us all, he made a comment that caused my perspective do a 180-degree turn. He said, 'Don't forget that the world is the context of our awakening and the crazier things become, the quicker we will all wake up.'

By 'wake up' Narain wasn't referring to physical sleep, but waking up spiritually: by seeing through our conditioning and rediscovering the true nature of ourselves and reality. Remember, within all of us is a permanently present awareness that isn't broken and resides beyond the temporary mental, emotional, physical and environmental stuff. This awareness is calm, loving and free – always – and losing connection with it causes us to get caught up in a world of conditioned, conflicting and constricting thoughts that then get projected outwards. As a result, many of the problems we see in the world are possible and perpetuated because we are asleep to the awareness within.

Wake-up calls

In the same way that we require an alarm to wake from a deep sleep, waking up spiritually requires something similar. Few people wake up when they are completely comfortable, when everything is perfect and going to their plan. Instead, we need wake-up calls that are suitably contrasting with the still, silent peaceful presence of our awareness, to stir us from sleepwalking through life. The world, right now, is the context we all need to wake up in. It is providing contrast from the inner calm and oneness, so that we can more easily find its presence within us.

Very encouragingly, if we look at the world, there are ever-increasing numbers of people commenting on how crazy things are and challenging the status quo. We are seeing movements that are questioning assumptions that have been held for generations. For example, a number of countries are currently legalizing gay marriage. This is something that was almost inconceivable 50 years ago. We've seen similar shifts in consciousness in other previously acceptable norms, such as slavery and unequal rights for women, during the past 100 years. We are questioning if the current breed of politicians and bankers have our best interests at heart and challenging the institutions that no longer serve society. Countless other norms are also being seen as not the kind of normal that we want and as a result, are starting to fall away. Humanity is waking up, and as we do, the outer is reflecting the new and improved inner. During this transition, do your best not to get disheartened by how things temporarily look.

We are evolving into a more awakened way of life.

New beginnings usually call for something to come to an end. Getting out of debt involves new spending habits, moving to a new home involves leaving the previous place, and embodying new behaviours requires the old ways of being to be relinquished. But how do we know when it's time to make a change? Life has a way of coming to a head so that we can see. Yes, the s**t may appear to be hitting the fan on many fronts, but it's fanning the flames of humanity getting clear on the kind of world we want to live in. The current state of affairs is therefore the fertilizer for a fresh new world to grow out of. Very often, when things appear to hit rock bottom, they turn out to be the exact wake-up call we need to clarify what we want and step towards it. Bring to mind a difficult time in your life. Now consider what it taught you and how it shaped you into the person you are today.

Wake-up calls like these are happening both personally and globally. With the passage of time and the benefit of hindsight, we can see that we may not be getting what we think we want, but being presented with exactly what we need.

USING CALM CURE ON COMMON WORLD ISSUES

Although the causes of the most significant world issues are complex and multifaceted, the blame game and the belief 'I can't make any meaningful difference,' are disempowering and ineffective for bringing about positive change. It's been said that if you don't believe something small can make a big impact, try spending the night in a room with a mosquito. You *can* make a big impact and now is the time to stop believing the contrary.

Consider some of the issues we all face on a day-to-day basis – from annoying neighbours and trying not to collide with people looking at their phone while walking down the street, to the state of the economy, the latest political crisis and even complex global issues such as poverty and climate change – and use Calm Cure on the one(s) that concern you most. In the same way that adding fire to fire doesn't help to extinguish it, bringing conflict to conflict is very similar. So it always pays to heal any conflict you may have in relation to these issues, to create the right inner foundation from which to start making a meaningful difference in the world.

 **TIP** *Go to www.calmclan.com/world for a FREE WORLD guided meditation.*

WAKING UP WILL HEAL THE WORLD

When I became a monk in 2008, I committed to healing humanity through the healing of myself. To this day it has been the most important commitment I have ever made. First, when I say 'waking up', remember that I don't mean from physical sleep. Instead, I'm referring to waking up spiritually by knowing the truth of who I am and experiencing oneness with divinity. If this sounds too 'out there' for your liking then may I suggest you explore any conditioning that would make you want to move away from experiencing pristine peace, unconditional joy, unbounded love and infinite freedom. This is because when you discover you are one with God (see note below), you also experience these stunning states too – as they are how the inner presence of God feels.

> **Note:** *Sometimes our conditioning can put us into conflict with the word 'God', so if you are uncomfortable with the word let me be clear: I am not referring to the concept of God of mainstream religion, but a presence that exists within everyone and everything. You are very welcome to substitute the word 'God' with Love, Life, Universe, Source, Nature, Divinity or any other word that works for you.*

No doubt you've experienced those moments in life – perhaps while watching a sunset or a bright full moon hanging low in the sky – when you've felt overwhelmed by the beauty of the world. It's at these times that we often feel at one with the world, totally in awe of the present moment, and also incredibly peaceful. And the reality is every one of us would like to feel this way all the time, to return to an experience of oneness with nature, the universe, with God. Even if we believe we only want a flash car, a house in the country or a promotion at work, it appears to be built into the fabric of humanity. Experiencing oneness with an inner source of peace, love, joy and freedom is awesome! I recommend it to everyone, especially those who want to bring about positive changes to the wider world.

Where is God? Hint: Not only in the sky!

As I touched upon earlier, the problems we see unfolding on the planet are a result of humanity putting God outside. If you were to ask most people: 'Where is God?', almost all of them would point to the sky. This belief that we are separate from God is the ultimate root cause of so much conflict. Two people *experiencing* peace do not fight over how peace is achieved. They happily hang out in harmony, knowing their peace stems from the same source. They also celebrate all superficial differences – race, religion, gender etc. – as they celebrate the spectrum of life.

Knowing that you, everyone you meet, and everything in the world is all made up of the same divine 'stuff', life becomes sacred. You don't resist what happens (because it is divine too) and you aren't attached to more or better (because you are filled up by an experience of 'the infinite'). You are complete, whole and at peace and nothing or no person or circumstance can take it away from you. You have a deep gratitude for life and are fully willing to experience the divine in its myriad of guises. Fear falls away as each moment is bathed in the light of love. This invincible love, that you now know you are, is no longer gained from other people, possessions or prestige, but is a wellspring from within, that is endless, pure and powerful.

Experiencing peace, love and perfection, you see the same reflected back from your life circumstances and the world. Naturally, you stop taking things so personally or seriously. Other people stop being so annoying or hurtful, even if they hold differences of opinion or act unconsciously in peculiar ways. Instead, you experience a courageous compassion and possess a deep desire for everyone to wake up from the conditioning that's causing them suffering. Life stops revolving around how you are feeling or if you are getting your own way. Knowing and experiencing the unified truth of reality, there is ultimately no individual 'you' to defend and life is an adventure; the world is the playground. You are flexible and free, incredibly content, recognize that the present moment *is* the gift, and live without limitations, as you go about fulfilling your divine purpose.

LIVING IN AN AWAKENED WORLD

Consider what the world would be like if everyone had *already* woken up? How would we treat the planet, if we knew it was nirvana, and how would we interact with one another if we knew we were all divine? Do you think the world would still have the same problems as it does today? Would there still be the need for war, if everyone (including the politicians and armies) were experiencing inner peace, love, joy and freedom within their own hearts and minds? It may all sound too good to be true or darn right impossible, but don't forget: if it's possible for the individual then the potential exists also for it to be possible for communities and countries. Don't give up on humanity too soon. We are just getting started! If you want to see this kind of world, it's up to *you* to be the change, now. Stop waiting for someone else to wake up first. It's your time and it's your turn. As one of the pioneers you do great service. Treading a new path, it's quicker and easier for the next person to wake up too.

> *'If not now, when? If not you, who?'*
> HILLEL THE ELDER

It almost goes without saying that I'm not about to attempt to explain in the last two paragraphs of this book how to discover your divinity. The main reason I raise this possibility now is because a) I genuinely believe as long as humanity remains asleep to the divinity within, then conflict in the world will continue; and b) the inner work you are doing with Calm Cure plays an important part in clearing the conditioning that prevents you from being consistently calm and living a full and free life.

The more conflicted you are, the more caught up in your mind you become, which fuels a separate sense of self and keeps you distracted from divinity. Calming the conditioned conflict, the attraction to overthinking dissolves, so allowing you more easily to be self-aware and experience a harmonious oneness with life. The state of the world is changing. Every day, an ever-increasing number of people are rediscovering their aware self and transcending the conflicts caused by their conditioning. Together, we are waking up to a new world, where humanity knows peace and lives free.

 TIP *For more support and free resources to apply the principles of Calm Cure to the WORLD, visit my Calm Clan: www.calmclan.com/world*

REFERENCES

1. news.harvard.edu/gazette/story/2010/11/wandering-mind-not-a-happy-mind; accessed 5 June 2015

2. www.conference-board.org/topics/publicationdetail.cfm?publicationid=3022

3. www.investorsinpeople.com/press/60-cent-uk-workers-not-happy-their-jobs

4. www.ons.gov.uk/employmentandlabourmarket/peopleinwork/employmentandemployeetypes/bulletins/uklabourmarket/february2016

5. www.statista.com/statistics/192342/unadjusted-monthly-number-of-part-time-employees-in-the-us/

6. www.marketwatch.com/story/this-is-how-much-money-exists-in-the-entire-world-in-one-chart-2015-12-18

7. www.theguardian.com/money/2015/oct/13/half-world-wealth-in-hands-population-inequality-report

8. www.gallup.com/poll/187982/americans-perceived-time-crunch-no-worse-past.aspx

9. journals.ama.org/doi/abs/10.1509/jmr.14.0130?journalCode=jmkr&

10. static.visionofhumanity.org/sites/default/files/GPI%202016%20Report_2.pdf

11. www.telegraph.co.uk/news/uknews/crime/12112024/Violent-crime-jumps-27-in-new-figures.html

THE CALM CURE
TECHNIQUE
AT A GLANCE

THE CALM CURE TECHNIQUE

Step 1. Clarify the Conflict
How does the condition/problem make me feel?

Describe your inner experience in one to five words/phrases.

- Where in my life have I felt this way?

- Recall a life event/circumstance when you've felt the same.

- What is happening that I do not want?

- State your root-cause resistance in one word/short phrase.

- What would I rather be experiencing instead?

This highlights your attachment(s) and when combined with the root-cause resistance creates the conflict experience.

Continue when you know your resistance and attachment.

Step 2. Calm Coexisting
Think/say: All things are possible and I am willing to experience [*state the attachment*] sometimes and I am willing to experience [*state the resistance*] sometimes.

- Rest into the willingness for both possibilities to coexist calmly within you and sometimes to show up in your life.

- On a scale of 0–10, with 10 being very high, how would I rate my willingness for both life experiences to happen?

If you rate below 10/10, go to step 3.

- On a scale of 0–10, with 10 being very high, how would I rate my 'peace with' experiencing the condition/situation?

If you rate below 10/10, go to step 3. When you rate 10/10 for both questions, you have calmed the conflict.

Step 3. Calm the Conflict

Calm Past

Recall a memory of a symbolic event when the root-cause resistance has shown up in your life, then ask:

- What can I know now, that if I had known in the past, I would never have resisted the event in the first place?

- Where do I feel these knowing(s) within my body? Imagine the movie of the memory, but this time looking through the eyes of a 'younger you' with the knowing(s) in that area of your body. Allow 30–60 seconds to do this.

- On a scale of 10–0, with 0 being 'the resistance is gone and I am at peace with it now', how would I rate the memory? If 0/10, repeat step 2. If above 0/10, proceed to Calm Future.

Calm Future

- Is it possible for me to be at peace with experiencing the root-cause resistance at some point in my life?

- What will the 'future me' know, to be at peace with it then?

- Where do I feel these knowing(s) within my body? Recall the memory of a symbolic event when the experience of the root-cause resistance has shown up in your life. Imagine the movie of the memory, but this time looking through the eyes of the 'older you' with the knowing(s) in that area of your body.

- On a scale of 10–0, with 0 being 'the resistance is gone and I am at peace with it now', how would I rate the memory?

If 0/10, repeat step 2. If you rate above 0/10, then return to step 1 to re-clarify the conflict, as you need to use the Calm Cure on a different conflict experience.

DIRECTORY OF 101 CONDITIONS AND THEIR CAUSES

Conditions and Mind-based causes	
Acne	Negativity towards self, comparison, feeling less than, lacking self-love, unaccepted, nervousness, unworthiness, unresolved pubescent event(s), perfectionistic, controlling, anger, 'There's something wrong with me'
Calm thought	I am lovingly gentle towards myself.
Acid reflux	Certain thing(s) hard to digest in relation to what you've witnessed and/or experienced, rejecting news, fear, anxiety, communication difficulties, anger about injustice, guilt and shame surrounding past action(s), self-doubt, acidic thinking
Calm thought	I am accepting of myself and life.
Allergies	Anger, unfriendly environment, unprotected, powerless, scared about getting in trouble, difficulty relaxing, unresolved hurt, blame/victim mentality, feeling controlled, unclear boundaries
Calm thought	I am friendly with the unfamiliar and responsible for how I respond to life.
Anaemia	Scared of what life might bring, expectation of difficulties arising, uneasy, worrisome thinking, unable to cope, questioning of abilities, feeling someone/something has 'drained the life' out of you, giving out without allowing yourself to receive back
Calm thought	I am joyfully facing life and assuming the best.

Conditions and Mind-based causes	
Appendicitis	Lacking inspiration in life, helpless, scared of what might happen, stuck unable to get away from toxic situation, angry, disappointed, loyalty conflict, let down by life, too hard on yourself
Calm thought	I am grateful for what I have and empowered to bring in even better.
Arthritis	Holding on, fixed ideas, identity attachment, anger, grief, resentment, giving out without getting back what you need, 'other people's goals more important than mine', unforgiveness, unresolved childhood rejections, unhappy with life but not doing anything about improving things
Calm thought	I am able to let go, let in the new and take action to be happy.
Asthma	Fear of death, unsupported in life, unable to cope, suppression of self, picking up on the stress and tension of parent or person close to you, undeserving of good things, need to prove worth, people-pleasing to get love
Calm thought	I am supported, deserving of the good and willing to say no when required.
Atherosclerosis	Feeling blocked, hard relationships, narrow-minded (but wouldn't want to admit it), limited range of feeling, disconnected from multifaceted self (for example, too physical, not enough spiritual), not going with the flow, separate, isolation
Calm thought	I am open-minded and -hearted and connected to my entire self.

Conditions and Mind-based causes	
Athlete's foot	Taking on board someone else's stale thinking/ways, anger at a perceived lack of love, feeling restricted and prevented from freely moving forward, looking outside for permission to act
Calm thought	I am accepted for who I am and free to move forwards with fresh ideas.
Auto-immune	Vulnerable, feeling attacked and/or under threat, inner conflict, unable to fight or run from external problem/threat, unsure who/what to trust, shutting down to protect, 'world is a dangerous place' mentality, overprotective, being hard on yourself
Calm thought	I am safe and protected within myself and the world.
Back pain (lower)	Unsupported, unable to support self, resistance and/or attachment to support others, unsafe, weak, vulnerable, incapable
Calm thought	I am supported, and willing and able to support myself and others.
Back pain (middle)	Disconnected from self, others and/or life force, threat from unseen source, hurt
Calm thought	I am connected to all aspects of myself.

Conditions and Mind-based causes	
Back pain (upper)	World on your shoulders, people-pleasing, carrying expectations, taking on other people's issues, unresolved pressing problem, suppressed, resistance to carry heavy problems/emotionally heavy people, attached to being carried
Calm thought	I am blessed by being able to carry myself and other people lightly.
Bacterial infection	Tired, fragile, vulnerable to being negatively impacted by other people and external events, feeling unloved/unsupported, stuck in a situation, angry at unfair treatment
Calm thought	I am strong and inwardly reliant and able to move into a happier space.
Bad breath	Personal space being invaded, desire to create separation, loner, past hurts leading to self-isolating tendencies, disgust towards inner voice
Calm thought	I am open to being close and to feeling connected to myself and others.
Bleeding gums	Unspoken insecurities, unnourished by others and life, angry and alone with a lack of support
Calm thought	I am secure and supported by life.
Burping (and also sneezing)	Unspoken thoughts about things you dislike, rejection of ideas, unresolved conflict(s) in relation to what you have recently consumed
Calm thought	I am free to speak my mind.

Conditions and Mind-based causes	
Cancer	Resistance to life, hurt, bitterness, anger, victim mentality, unforgiveness, guilt, grief, regret, perceived lack of love, out of control, unresolved past hurts, invaded, hiding and resistance to true feelings, attached to a different life
Calm thought	I am free to forgive and I love life in a loving and compassionate world.
Candida	Vulnerable, invaded, untrusting, imbalance between taking and giving, feeding off others, doubt, anger towards an irritating person/situation
Calm thought	I am able to forgive and feed my own needs.
Coeliac disease	Judgemental, good vs. bad thinking, attached to good, resisting bad, sensitive to external influences, unable to cope with criticism, self-dislike, unable to digest being unheard/uncared about, hiding true thoughts/feelings, unseen
Calm thought	I am accepting and allowing, and release the need for others to nourish me.
Chronic pain	Anger, resentment, resisting emotions, not being honest or feeling true feelings, things left unsaid and/or unfelt, unforgivingness
Calm thought	I am free to feel and speak my feelings.
Colds	Overwhelmed, overworking, fast-paced nonstop living, uncertainty, confusion, escaping environmental negativity
Calm thought	I am safe when I slow down and rest.

Conditions and Mind-based causes	
Cold sores	Feeling run-down, uncommunicative, concerns around being accepted, awkwardness, feeling controlled by others and let down by life
Calm thought	I am accepted for who I am and able to feel comfortable when showing myself.
Colitis	Hurt, helpless, sad, confused, 'what's the point?' mentality, want external help instead of helping yourself, unable to process or comprehend what's happened, holding on to painful past
Calm thought	I am free from past hurts and able to help myself heal and be happy.
Conjunctivitis	Fear of what might happen, worry, resisting the fear that you are seen in a negative light
Calm thought	I am loved always, with love being the unseen connector within all of life.
Constipation	Undecided, holding on, fear of not having enough, ungratefulness, loss, resisting change, hoarding, giving what you need, uncomfortable to receive, stuck in worrisome thinking pattern, scared about what might happen
Calm thought	I am grateful for having enough and make courageous decisions.
Cough	Feeling unseen and/or unheard, barking at life, feeling left out, unable to ask for what you want or need, ignoring issues, irritation at self and others, inaction
Calm thought	I am included, important and able to make positive changes.

Conditions and Mind-based causes	
Dandruff	Feeling sucked dry by pressures, people and/or responsibilities, too many things to do, overworking, people-pleasing, hiding true feelings relating to how stressed you feel, suffering in silence
Calm thought	I am capable of meeting the demands of my day and do what's comfortable.
Deafness	Resistance and/or rejection to what you are hearing/have heard, more interested in your inner world than external world, overloaded by negativity, unresolved past events where you've heard upsetting things, feeling unheard and/or controlled by others, unwilling to receive guidance
Calm thought	I am receiving my inner and outer world loud and clear.
Dermatitis	Highly critical towards self and others, anger, feeling concerned and stressed about external life and circumstances, rejection of environment, feeling used and/or violated
Calm thought	I am accepting of my world and calm with my circumstances.
Depression	Thinking about life instead of living, lack of compelling purpose, pointlessness, resistance to feeling fully to the point of numbness, unseen, overthinking, 'surviving life is difficult' thoughts
Calm thought	I deserve the good in life and let 'what is' be good enough.

Conditions and Mind-based causes	
Diabetes	Lacking sweetness, numb, bored, taking on parents' problems, frequently feeling let down, self-suppression, wanting more from life but unsure how to get it, fear, lacking compelling purpose, judgement instead of joy, effort to exist
Calm thought	I am the sweetness I want and worthy of being myself fully.
Diarrhoea	Emotional upset, strategy for getting away/avoiding, angry at being told what to do, perceived lack of choice, escaping, uncertainty surrounding choices, fear, rejecting before you are rejected
Calm thought	I am free to choose what feels safe and do what I want.
Diverticulitis	Unexpressed non-acceptance, anger and agitation about what life has given you, resistance to 'what is' and attachment to something else happening, controlling, 'My way or no way'
Calm thought	I am accepting of what is and open to new ways of being and doing.
Dizziness	Imbalanced, ungrounded, loss of stability, don't know where you stand, too in your head, disconnected from body, resistance to uncertainty
Calm thought	I am grounded within my still stable self.

Conditions and Mind-based causes	
Dystonia	Constricting inner power, scared of own strength, shame about things you shouldn't have done, scared of hurting others, conflict towards completion, 'I can't do it' attitude
Calm thought	I am free to use my strength and commit to completing.
Earache	Not listening to inner voice, rejection of what you are hearing from external sources, protecting yourself by trying to ignore what you are hearing, closed to other opinions and ideas, annoyance
Calm thought	I am open to hearing opinions knowing I am a good person.
Eczema	Sadness-based anger, alone in the world, skin trying to find lost connection, isolated, irritated, emotionally sensitive, unstable without physical contact, separation anxiety
Calm thought	I am calm and connected.
Endometriosis	Closed off to love, need for pity, sexual shame, intimacy vulnerability, anger, feeling misunderstood or undervalued, attachment or resistance to past sexual partner(s), resistance to rejection
Calm thought	I am open to connecting deeply.

Conditions and Mind-based causes	
Fatigue	Unable to fight or get away from something stressful/scary and/or negative, feeling suppressed, overwhelmed, chronic resistance, rejecting life before it rejects you again
Calm thought	I am accepting of my inner power.
Flatulence	Difficulty digesting inner thoughts or external events, inner concern, keeping things to yourself, feeling undecided
Calm thought	I am able to make decisions and digest what's happened and happening.
Fungal infections	Stale thinking, acting against your inner knowing/heart, relationship secrets that make you feel unclean, holding on to a past that no longer serves you today
Calm thought	I am fresh in my thinking and free of the past.
Gallstones	Unresolved hurt(s), loss, feeling like you should have done more with your life, anger towards self, unforgiveness
Calm thought	I am at peace with what's happened and capable of creating.
Glandular fever	Feeling unwanted, anger and hurt towards a perceived lack of love, 'If nobody else cares why should I?' mentality, tired of trying to prove loveability, dejected, unable to express, resistance to feeling inner emotions fully
Calm thought	I am loved and wanted and am willing to feel and be me.

Conditions and Mind-based causes	
Haemorrhoids	Holding on, emotionally uncomfortable with choices you've made, unsure what to do next, feeling under pressure, unforgiving towards self and others
Calm thought	I am at peace with past choices and open to knowing and doing what's best.
Hair loss	Feeling vulnerable, unprotected, fear of the unknown, prolonged stress, underlying frustrations, resistance to feminine aspects of self
Calm thought	I am safe and calmly face anything that comes my way.
Hay fever	Environmental threats, rejecting or questioning your place on Earth, guilt, resistance to receive, resisting location, lacking space, fighting feelings
Calm thought	I am happy where I am with space to think, feel and be still.
Headaches	Something on your mind, overthinking, denial, guilt, shame, regret, self-suppression, deserving of punishment, invasion of space, angry thoughts
Calm thought	I am accepting of myself and life.
Heart disease	Hurt, closed-off, sadness, ignoring the needs of the physical, emotional and/or spiritual aspects of your self, divided, disconnected, hard relationships
Calm thought	I am open to all aspects of myself.

Conditions and Mind-based causes	
Herpes	Belief of being 'bad', sexual shame, deserving of punishment, needing excuse to avoid intimacy, feeling used, violated or unclean
Calm thought	I am a good person with pure intentions.
Hives	Angry and irritated with self, others and/or life, overwhelmed by feelings and/or circumstances, fear, helplessness
Calm thought	I am calm and at peace with myself, others and my environment.
Hyperhidrosis	Anger, irritated, unfairness, resistance to being in the hot seat and the centre of attention, need to cool down mentally and emotionally, unresolved shock, scared of own strength
Calm thought	I am cool with being the centre of attention and calm about the past.
Hypertension	Resistance, worry, anxiety, belief the world is a dangerous place, controlling, not safe to relax, unwilling to let go, attached to things happening 'my way'
Calm thought	I am at peace with how the world is.

Conditions and Mind-based causes	
Hyperthyroidism	Resistance to maintaining status quo, need to get going, nervous tension, anxiety, irritability, feeling held back and/or being/doing what you need to do, desire to move forwards but feeling blocked, pressure from responsibilities, questioning readiness to support self, feeling forced to grow up too quickly
Calm thought	I am free to make progress towards my purpose at a peaceful pace.
Hypotension	Drained by attachments, not getting what you want, tired of trying, negativity around own abilities and purpose, belief that nobody is there for me, what's the point if nobody cares?
Calm thought	I am passionate about going for my purpose without needing it.
Hypothyroidism	Unsafe, unable to cope, weak, vulnerable, too much to deal with, resisting a perceived lack of support in past or present, resistance to responsibilities, need to retreat to protect and feel safe, 'Life is hard', 'I can't do this' and/or 'What's the point?'
Calm thought	I am capable of coping with life and more supported than I may think.

Conditions and Mind-based causes	
Infections	Feeling vulnerable to external attack, overpowered by external influences, low defences, unable to cope, anger towards nobody noticing your difficulties, prolonged pressure to perform, tired of trying so hard
Calm thought	I am able to cope and give myself permission to be at ease and enjoy life.
Infertility	Imbalance between masculine and feminine energies, resistance to receiving and/or creating, feeling inadequate, unresolved past fears around falling pregnant, unresolved issues with parent(s), avoidance of and fears around making the same mistakes your parents did or having similar experiences
Calm thought	I am balanced in my ability to give and receive and thankful for what my parents have taught me.
Influenza	Too much external negativity, weak and vulnerable, running on empty, finding it hard to carry responsibilities, wanting to get away from it all, needing to justify taking time off/get away
Calm thought	I am free to take time for myself to rest and let go of extra responsibilities.
Insomnia	Not safe to switch off, need to stay alert, ignoring unresolved events, undeserving of the reward of rest, over-compromising, unheard heart
Calm thought	I am at peace with being peaceful.

Conditions and Mind-based causes	
Irritable bowel syndrome (IBS)	Irritated, unable to process, comprehend or understand, fear, emotional upset, untrusting, holding on to out-of-date thinking, uncertainty conflict between needing to let go/get away and holding on to what no longer serves, attached
Calm thought	I am clear-minded, light-hearted and pursue my purpose with positivity.
Itching	Anger, irritation, hot-headedness, self-punishment, shame, hiding secrets that sit below the surface, worry, angst
Calm thought	I am secure within the skin I'm in.
Kidney infection	Feeling upset, bitter, impure, holding on to negativity, fear, unsafe, perceived threats to your boundaries, low confidence, powerless due to exhaustion, tired of trying
Calm thought	I am confident and able to maintain healthy boundaries.
Kidney stone	Fear-based anger, lacking trust, the need to become hardened in order to protect yourself and feel safe, set in your ways, focused on the past to the detriment of the present and the future, feeling 'less than', pressure to perform
Calm thought	I am trusting that I am safe and take positive action into new territory.

Conditions and Mind-based causes	
Lips (dry/cracked)	Unconfident, scared to look stupid, be rejected and make a fool of yourself, nervousness, questioning abilities to deliver, uncertainty around what you are saying
Calm thought	I am carefree around what people think and believe in my abilities to deliver.
Menopausal symptoms	Buying into cultural beliefs around ageing, suppressed anger and frustration, resisting loss of youthfulness and/or desirability
Calm thought	I am loving life as an ageless goddess.
Migraines	Resistance to unfair events, guilt, regret, shame, self-punishment, invasion of space, shutting the world out, unable to ask for what you need, safer to be sick than face the world, unable to cope, denial, grief
Calm thought	I am capable with a good heart.
Mouth ulcer	Anger eating away at you, not expressing personal opinions, resistance to what you are thinking or saying, holding in frustration, attached to old thinking habits that promote problems rather than peace
Calm thought	I am open to new perspectives that allow me to be at peace.
Mumps	Overthinking, ignoring/going against inner knowing, unable to say what you think, instability, status quo challenged, uncertain, fear of the unknown
Calm thought	I am comfortable with uncertainly and can rely on my inner knowing.

Conditions and Mind-based causes	
Myalgic encephalopathy (ME)	Resistance towards and fighting life, viewing life as a struggle, anger due to feelings of unfairness, unexpressed thoughts/feelings, retreating from responsibilities, under pressure to fulfil commitments, unable to fight or get away from stressful person/situation
Calm thought	I am free to be and do what I want and at peace with what life brings.
Nausea	Confusion, constant questioning, feeling out of control, unable to receive what you want/need, rejection of information and/ or an unwanted experience, holding a poisonous perspective, sick to the stomach about something or someone, ungrounded
Calm thought	I am stable in what I know is right.
Numbness	Unwilling to feel feelings fully, untrusting of instincts and intuition, unresolved emotions from the past, detached from aspects of yourself
Calm thought	I am willing to feel fully and trust my instincts and intuitions.
Osteoporosis	Inflexibility, rigid thinking, fixed ideas, unwilling to change, lack of structure, unable to support self, weak from supporting others, feeling inferior, bitterness, hate, resistance to standing up for yourself and/or attachment to external source of structure/support
Calm thought	I am flexible and stand strongly in love.

Conditions and Mind-based causes	
Parasites	Negativity, powerless, feeling people/ events are feeding off your energy, invaded, unclear boundaries, imbalance between giving and receiving (less gained than given), imbalance
Calm thought	I am empowered by having balance between giving and receiving.
Parkinson's disease	Moving fearfully through life, unresolved past events that caused panic, stuck energy, feeling stuck in situations, conflicted between what's right for you and what's best for others, hiding and suppressing your true feelings
Calm thought	I am free and express my true feelings.
Period pains	Resistance to not being pregnant, grief, anger, unresolved emotions relating to around the time in life when periods first started, resistance to female roles and responsibilities, 'not fair' mentality
Calm thought	I am at peace with letting go.
Pneumonia	Unsupported by life, looking outside for sustenance, alone, isolated, drained by daily duties, unwilling or unable to face life challenges, feeling restricted, closed
Calm thought	I am supported by life and able to stand strongly when faced with challenges.

Conditions and Mind-based causes	
Polymyalgia rheumatica	Rigid thinking, unwilling to accept other viewpoints, frustrated that your viewpoints are unheard, not listening to or acting upon inner voice, carrying heavy responsibilities, 'what's the point' mentality, feeling controlled, unable to make progress towards what you want
Calm thought	I am open-minded, share my opinions without attachment and am able to make progress.
Prostate	Feeling taken over or controlled, conflicts around getting older, intrusion of work or personal space, status quo challenged
Calm thought	I am secure with my space in the world.
Psoriasis	Feeling bullied, unprotected, vulnerable, fear, need extra-thick line of defence, unresolved near-death experience, hurt
Calm thought	I am protected and powerful.
Raynaud's disease	Ignoring/closed off to aspects of yourself and life, not going with the flow, isolated, disconnected, alone
Calm thought	I am going with the flow and open to all aspects of myself and life.
Shingles	Highly sensitive, unable to cope and/or keep up with demands, concerns relating to circumstances, environmental fears, masculine/feminine imbalance (depending on side of body the symptoms are showing)
Calm thought	I am at peace within myself and comfortable with circumstances.

Conditions and Mind-based causes	
Sinusitis	Frustration towards self, others and/or environmental concerns, feeling blocked with a desire to run away, facing life with a lack of tenderness, unable to select/choose between multiple options, indecision, fear of getting it wrong due to unresolved emotions relating to perceived past mistakes
Calm thought	I am at peace with the world, trusting of my instincts and choose what's right.
Snoring	Not feeling heard, things on your mind that remain unsaid, holding back from taking the action you know you need to take, fear of the new, stuck in ways
Calm thought	I am free to be and do what I want.
Sore throat	Not speaking truth, holding thoughts and feelings in, 'What I have to say doesn't matter or make a difference'
Calm thought	I am free to speak my mind.
Stomach pain and bloating	Indigestible news, unable to process or understand, things unsaid/unfelt, suppression of true thoughts/feelings
Calm thought	I am welcoming of unexpected news and I am honest with myself and others.
Stye (eye)	Losing sight of someone or something you love dearly, feeling separated, loss of love, confusion, scared, disoriented, unresolved anger and disappointment
Calm thought	I am open to love from new sources.

Conditions and Mind-based causes	
Teeth grinding	Responsibilities playing on your mind, bitten off more than you can chew, worry, anger, hidden desire to bite out, indecision, processing something
Calm thought	I am clear on what to do and will do it with calmness and confidence.
Thrush	Angry and irritated towards self about past decisions and actions, upset with partner, self-judgemental, self-critical, feeling invaded by other people's ideas, opinions or needs, ignoring own needs
Calm thought	I am at peace with my past decisions.
Tinnitus	Rejection of what you are saying to yourself or what you have heard, isolation, lost in your own world, resistance to silence or sound
Calm thought	I am engaged with life and eager to hear.
Tonsillitis	Not speaking truth, protecting secrets, guilt, fear of being found out, need to put defences up, suppressing self, feeling frustrated and/or stifled
Calm thought	I am imperfectly perfect like everyone else.
Tumours	Hurts, emotional wounds, unresolved trauma and/or shock, inner conflict caused by jealousy towards others and not believing it's possible for you and/or not feeling deserving/worthy
Calm thought	I am worthy of calm and completeness.

Conditions and Mind-based causes	
Ulcers	Something eating away at you, bitter, acidic thinking/feeling, pushing down, resentment in your responsibilities
Calm thought	I am allowing of life.
Warts	Anger due to an event that made you feel scared, extra-thick defence against singular event, feeling incapable, ugly
Calm thought	I am at peace with no need to protect.
Water retention	Relationship problems, sadness, overflowing with emotions, feeling stagnant, need for the new, not making the changes you know you need to make, holding back from being happy
Calm thought	I am in flow with my feelings and open to knowing how to be happy.
Weight gain	Unprotected, unsafe, unfamiliar and/or unfriendly environment(s), no control, hiding, withholding true feelings, unable to cope, loss of comfort, harsh self-speak that body needs to protect itself from, lack of self-love/acceptance
Calm thought	I am surrendering to how my delicious destiny is being revealed to me.
Weight loss	Dissatisfaction, unfed by life, undeserving of nourishment, cry for help, controlling, vulnerable, unresolved resistance to lack of support, unable to take what you need, unworthy, shame, 'It's my fault' mentality
Calm thought	I am nourished and deserving of the good in life.

Conditions and Mind-based causes	
Verrucas	Angry at self, guilt, something eating away at you, secret(s), needing to take action but letting fear stop you, feeling ungrounded due to the confusion arising from the multiple options available
Calm thought	I am at peace with myself and am willing to do what I know I need to do.
Viruses	External environmental issues (making you feel vulnerable, invaded, attacked, unfairly 'got at'), under pressure, scared and/or stuck, feeling unable to fight, unprotected, living in a state of high alert, inability to relax, inner unease
Calm thought	I am safe and protected and can keep calm amid challenging circumstances.
Voice loss	Unheard, what you say doesn't matter, powerless to make a positive difference, ignoring your inner voice, feeling unable to fully express your feelings
Calm thought	I am heard and know what I feel is important even if others don't appear to listen.
Yeast infections	Feeling invaded by other people's ideas, opinions or needs, ignoring own needs, lack of self-love and respect
Calm thought	I am able to think whatever I want.

TOP TIP: FREE ONLINE SUPPORT

An online version of this Conditions Directory is available at www.sandynewbigging.com/calmdirectory. A further four directories are also available in my book, Body Calm, including ones listing the common causes of issues relating to the Body Parts, Organs, Systems and Senses.

Next Steps

STRESS-FREE,
SUPER-SUCCESSFUL LIVING

CALM CLAN

My Calm Clan is your online resource for meditation, holistic health, and living fully and freely. As a member you get unlimited access to 100+ hours of teaching videos, exclusive guided meditations and monthly live broadcasts with me, my team of Calmologists and guest experts. This is a great way to get the support you need in meditation and life. Start your 30-day free trial today.
www.calmclan.com

CALM ACADEMY

My Calm Academy offers a home-study certification course in Calmology, which is the combination of my Mind Calm, Body Calm and Calm Cure techniques. Millions of people crave more calm in their lives and are waiting to learn meditation and experience the Calm Cure from you! Train as a Calmologist with my Academy to study at home and change the world!
www.calmacademy.com

CALM RETREATS

I run retreats where you can enjoy the benefits of my Calmology principles and techniques. During a long weekend in the UK or a longer retreat at my international venues, you will have the opportunity to learn meditation from my team and me, which will help deepen your understanding and experience of the techniques.

CALM COURSES

I run one-day and weekend courses sharing the Calmology principles and techniques, including Mind Calm, Body Calm and Calm Cure. They are fun and also offer a deeper understanding and experience of what's been shared in this book.

ASCENSION COURSES

My original meditation technique is known as Ascension, as taught by the Ishayas of The Bright Path. I am an Ishaya Monk and qualified teacher of the Ascension techniques. I credit much of what I've learned about peace, freedom and conscious living to my Ascension practice and guidance from my Spiritual Teacher, M.K.I. I highly recommend you learn to 'ascend' if you have a desire to know what it means to be truly alive and would value a path that can help you to wake up and be free.

For more info about my retreats and courses, an online version of the Conditions Directory and additional free resources on the topics covered within this book, visit my website: **www.sandynewbigging.com**

ABOUT THE AUTHOR

Angie Peach Vasquez

Sandy C. Newbigging is the creator of the Mind Detox, Mind Calm, Body Calm and Calm Cure techniques – collectively known as Calmology. He has written several bestselling books, including *Heal the Hidden Cause*, *Life Detox*, *Mind Calm* and *Body Calm*. His work has been seen on a number of TV channels including Discovery Health. To work with Sandy you can either join his Calm Clan membership site, train as a Calmologist via his Calm Academy or experience one-to-one coaching.

Sandy was recently commended by the Federation of Holistic Therapists as Tutor of the Year. He was called 'The Mind Maestro' by *Psychologies* magazine and described by *Yoga Magazine* as 'one of the best meditation teachers around'. For more information about Sandy or to book him for a speaking event, please use the following contact details:

 answers@sandynewbigging.com

 sandycnewbigging

 sandynewbigging

 sandynewbigging

www.sandynewbigging.com

We hope you enjoyed this Hay House book. If you'd like to receive our online catalog featuring additional information on Hay House books and products, or if you'd like to find out more about the Hay Foundation, please contact:

Hay House, Inc., P.O. Box 5100, Carlsbad, CA 92018-5100
(760) 431-7695 or (800) 654-5126
(760) 431-6948 (fax) or (800) 650-5115 (fax)
www.hayhouse.com® • www.hayfoundation.org

• • •

Published and distributed in Australia by: Hay House Australia Pty. Ltd., 18/36 Ralph St., Alexandria NSW 2015 • Phone: 612-9669-4299 • Fax: 612-9669-4144
www.hayhouse.com.au

Published and distributed in the United Kingdom by: Hay House UK, Ltd., Astley House, 33 Notting Hill Gate, London W11 3JQ • Phone: 44-20-3675-2450 • Fax: 44-20-3675-2451
www.hayhouse.co.uk

Published and distributed in the Republic of South Africa by: Hay House SA (Pty), Ltd., P.O. Box 990, Witkoppen 2068 • info@hayhouse.co.za • www.hayhouse.co.za

Published in India by: Hay House Publishers India, Muskaan Complex, Plot No. 3, B-2, Vasant Kunj, New Delhi 110 070 • Phone: 91-11-4176-1620 • Fax: 91-11-4176-1630
www.hayhouse.co.in

Distributed in Canada by: Raincoast Books, 2440 Viking Way, Richmond, B.C. V6V 1N2 • Phone: 1-800-663-5714 • Fax: 1-800-565-3770 • www.raincoast.com

• • •

Take Your Soul on a Vacation

Visit www.HealYourLife.com® to regroup, recharge, and reconnect with your own magnificence. Featuring blogs, mind-body-spirit news, and life-changing wisdom from Louise Hay and friends.

Visit www.HealYourLife.com today!